PRAYER
THE CATALYST FOR CLIMATE CHANGE

Apostle Steve Lyston

Edited by: Marsha A. McCormack

1

DEDICATION

This book is dedicated to God, our Creator, who created for us a perfect planet.

This book is also dedicated to the true intercessor who pray for the planet.

This book is further dedicated to those who want to know and understand the truth about our planet and to organizations and nations who truly want to give resources to poorer countries who have challenges in meeting the sustainable development goals despite the disaster they experience.

Finally, this book is dedicated to the environmentalists and those who work assiduously toward the betterment of the planet.

THANK YOU

To the Holy Spirit for granting the inspiration, foresight and insight in this work.

To my wife, Michelle Lyston and to our children Shevado Lyston, Hannah Lyston and Joshua Lyston for the sacrifices you made so that this book (and all others) could come forth.

To Petagaye Jolly and Letisha Livingstone for their help in preparing this work.

To Jasmine Calixte for your encouragement and support during this project.

To Bishop Dr. Doris Hutchinson for your continued, unwavering support.

To Marsha McCormack and Johann Williams for being a great support team.

TABLE OF CONTENTS

Page #

PRAYERS, DECREES AND DECLARATIONS

INTRODUCTION

In order to understand Climate Change, we must get back to the foundational truths found in the Book of Genesis, where God created a perfect world.

We should not fear when it comes to Climate Change, because within the scriptures are found the do's and don'ts, the solutions and how it all ends. The original order of man's environment on the earth must be distinguished from what it became following the impact of man's fall, the curse and the eventual deluge affecting flora, fauna and mankind throughout the planet.

God is not the One to be blamed for our planet's current status. He created it for man's enjoyment, but the sin of man has created death and disaster.

Despite the great flood we read about in the Bible, man's heart and way of thinking have not changed much and is evident in man's treatment of the planet at large.

For climate change to take place, man must examine his heart and engage in a heart change. So, we must begin to "love thy neighbor as you love yourself; and abstain from greed and begin to reduce the weapons of mass destruction.

After the first flood, that changed the course of the earth environmentally and the very animals were affected. God made a covenant with man and sealed that promise with a sign – the rainbow (Genesis 9: 12 – 15). That rainbow was the sign of Promise and symbolic of The Promise of Grace – Jesus Christ; to let man know that He would never destroy the earth again by water, but instead by fire next time. (2 Peter 3: 10). He lets us know that He has made a promise that He WILL keep. Ultimately, Jesus is the "App" for Climate Change. Once you accept Him by faith.

Sin is what affects creation. Only the Creator must be worshipped. Psalm 148 tells us that the entire creation must worship Him as the Creator – Sun, Moon, Man, Stars, Heaven of Heavens, Water, Angels must all worship Him.

We ought not to focus completely on some of the scientific predictions – water vapor and greenhouse effect and so on. We must instead focus on Truth, Righteousness, Peace, Helping the Poor and Fair Distribution of Resources, True Justice – then will we see global change.

We also need to read the Book of Revelation that speaks of Apocalyptic events which will take place in the End-Time. This will guide scientists on how to proceed and the precautions that need to be taken by the globe, that we may achieve the sustainable development goals and save lives.

Chapter 1

CLIMATE CHANGE: WORLD CRISIS AND APOCALYPTIC EVENT

Climate change affects everyone and daily life in general, at every level, in every sector of our society; from the newborn to national economies, and impacts our decision-making more than we can imagine.

The term "**Climate**" refers to "*the weather condition, prevailing in the area in general or over a long period; atmospheric condition or region with particular prevailing condition; the prevailing trend of public opinion or of another.*" So, it clearly goes beyond weather patterns.

UN Chief Antonio Guterres called on governments "... to stop building new coal plants by 2020, cut greenhouse emissions by 45% over the next decade and overhauling fossil fuel-driven economies with new technologies like solar and wind. The world," he said, "is facing a grave climate emergency."

The heat waves that have been occurring in different parts of the globe are cause for concern; and this will negatively affect the poor, especially regarding health costs and energy consumption. The homeless who have no shelter will also be negatively and directly affected. There needs to be emergency funding made available to the poor.

Now is the time funding and subsidies should be made available to the poor and to those in rural areas. This will help small businesses to cope with the high energy costs that will arise.

The priority must now be to plant more trees and relocate those who are closer to highly forested areas in order to prevent tragedy through fires. Nations also need to establish more water wells to deal with this crisis, as the excessive heat will require more water usage. Furthermore, the ground water will disappear and we have the opportunity now to collect it before it does. What has happened in India - where its sixth (6th) largest city has run out of water with almost ten (10) million people are without water - should be a lesson to us all.

Tourism Fallout

Nations need to stop the lip service and begin to put serious emergency plans in place, especially for tourism fallout. This is especially true for the Caribbean and Latin American nations.

More people will want to go to cooler destinations. Places like Russia, Alaska, Norway, Holland and their tourism numbers will begin to increase as the world weather crisis will intensify. This is not good for the investors.

The water shortage has the potential to affect hotels, prisons, schools, hospitals, shelters. It can also affect airports and trigger shutdowns.

Urgent plans need to be put in place to prevent the spread of disease, particularly where the viruses or bacteria thrive in heat.

Also, additional Fire Trucks, Water Storage Tanks and improved water facilities, as well as portable tanks are needed, as the poor, small children and the elderly are always the most vulnerable.

Farmers

It was reported that during the 2018-2019 winter (1 October 2018 – 1 April 2019), an estimated 37.7% of managed honey bee colonies in the United States were lost. Honey supply to producers of cereals, some medicines and drinks is significantly affected.

Contingencies and emergency plans need to be put in place for farmers because the heat and the floods as well as hail and the wintry weathers have the potential to seriously and irreversible affect the Agricultural Industry, Livestock and the Fishing Industry.

Water Facilities

More Water Parks need to be set up for children to make use of as they play outside. It will keep them hydrated and less susceptible to the heat waves. Further to this, there is technology that allows water to be pumped every time children use the playground and that is something worth looking into, if we are serious about addressing this crisis.

In addition to all this, we must remember that this kind of crisis has the potential to push up already rising oil prices, food costs and practically every cost that we can incur as human beings. So, it is a dire situation that needs to be addressed with great urgency.

Divine Intervention

We cannot address Climate Change unless we decide to include the One Who made the climate. Luke 21: 25 – 26, 2 Corinthians 7:13, 2 Kings 8: 35 - 36 and Revelation 16: 21 speak to us about the distress within the earth especially regarding Climate

Change. There are also things that we need to know which affect Climate Change. For example, Prayer has a positive effect on the climate; as does Atonement. Most countries are trying to legislate the Creator out of their nation.

During such urgent times, the focus ought not to be on dealing with the climatic issues through science only; but we must include a wider cross-section of individuals and deal with the matter holistically.

Apocalyptic Nature

With all the great effort being made by various nations to address the issue of climate change, and awareness that the media is attempting to bring to the topic, there are some key elements that are missing in addressing what is taking place.

Despite man's best efforts, we cannot separate the natural, scientific and spiritual connection that exists between man, the entire Universe, and God. Luke 21: 25 says, "And there will be signs in the sun, in the moon, and in the stars; and on the earth distress of nations, with perplexity, the sea and the waves roaring;"

We are seeing these six (6) occurrences taking place in the earth like never before. The "Red Tide" in parts of Florida, earthquakes in diverse places, volcanic eruptions, floods displacing hundreds of thousands of people, hurricanes occurring close to places that do not usually get such happenings, rare fire tornadoes and other fires raging all over the world, and the Pacific Ocean being 10 degrees warmer than usual. All these together have the potential to bring about a global famine (Food and Water will be the new gold.)

Man's Contribution

Negative declarations/words, as well as alternative lifestyles, greed, unrighteousness, crime, violence, abortion, witchcraft, the worship of the universe and its contents instead of the Creator all have their consequential effect on the earth (Psalm 148). Man has to remember that the very Universe depends on the Creator for its function and sustenance. Injustice, breaking Spiritual laws, and the way we treat the poor are just as important and consequential.

Science

If the Bible tells us that God is shortening the day for the sake of the elect, then it also means that the earth's axis would also be shifted. That would affect every aspect of nature. The creation of the Universe occurred by the Word spoken by God. Any repairing or restoration that would take place must be through the Word. Hebrews 11: 3 reminds us of this – look more deeply at the word "framed" in that Scripture.

Whenever we try to legislate God's Word out of our schools, workplaces and the environment, it will impact negatively on the climate. Man's actions affect the earth, the climate, the air, the ocean, and very soon will cause a greater problem with our local and global communication systems.

God created a perfect climate/cosmos. However, man's actions created a negative impact. Similarly, God created the rainbow – a symbol to man that He is the scientific "cure" for the earth and all within.

When we cut down our trees and don't replace them, or run toxic waste into the rivers and oceans, or interfere with the atmosphere, then we will continue to have more problems.

When we erect altars and statues to worship instead of worshipping the Almighty Creator, it will negatively affect us.

Apocalyptic Events

To truly understand what is happening we must first begin to understand the Book of Revelation. The

Seven Seals and the Seven Trumpets which will unfold. Revelation 7, 8 and 9, these Scriptures speak of the different horses – black, pale, white and gray which speak of economic disruption and inflation which will trigger global famine. They also symbolize disaster, death, oceanic contamination, skin disease, water and food related sicknesses, starvation, devastation, military conflict, communication problems, cosmic catastrophes – which would affect the seven structures of creation and the seven classes of men and cause agricultural, horticultural and aqua-cultural problems. Then we would see freak storms and winds. All vegetation will be affected as well. We are seeing more frequent occurrence of falling meteoroids which will destroy much of the marine life and marine commerce.

There is going to be pollution of fresh water (Revelation 8: 10 - 11)

For years I have been calling for strategic plans for storage of water and food, and for the protection of natural waters particularly in the Developing Countries – like Jamaica, which is also called the Land of Wood and Water. Storage of water and food will be critical and we cannot continue to look at climate change from a singular perspective.

Chapter 2

GOD CONTROLS THE CLIMATE

In my view, Climate Change concerns/includes whatever you allow to take place in your environment, airspace, zone – good or bad, spiritually or naturally. It is for us critical, therefore, to know the character and plans of those who takes dominion over and within our communities and nation. What we permit or forbid is critical to the health of our community. If we permit abortion, sexual immorality and witchcraft to take dominion over the area, for example, that will have a negative impact on our society overall. There are many, who are deemed experts on climate change, who speak about this topic at length. But the questions we need to ask are:

Are they being truthful or honest in their reports and regarding the topics they discuss? Is it about shifting wealth from one to the other?

Is it a plan to shift our focus from what the Word of God says about the climate? That topic is clear in the Scriptures. After all, He created and controls the climate.

Real Christians should not be afraid of Climate Change, God controls the weather. Psalm 46: 2 – 3 reminds us, "Therefore we will not fear, even though the earth be removed, and though the mountains be carried into the midst of the sea; though its waters roar and be troubled, though the mountains shake with its swelling." So, we are not to fear despite the earthquake, tornados, landslides, volcanic eruptions that we experience.

Why are we worrying about the greenhouse effects, gas emissions and the burning of coal? In earlier days, the burning of coal was more frequently done and the people then were healthier than those now. We didn't have 5G and 4G or cell sites then and now we are less healthy. In addition to this, "Swiss and German scientists also suggested that increasing radiation from the sun may be responsible for part of the recent warming" and the excessive heat. They say the sun is getting brighter. How would the scientists explain Revelation 16: 9 "And men were scorched with great heat, and they blasphemed the name of God who has power over these plagues; and they did not repent and give Him glory."

John 4: 8 and Luke 12: 55 speak about the South wind which would bring increased heat and high temperatures upon man. This heat will also cause melting of ice and flooding in other regions. (See also Psalm 19: 6, **Isaiah** 49: 10 and Job 24: 19) These are facts that God control climate.

Furthermore, the danger will increase because during the heat the vipers and snakes begin to surface even more.

It is God who controls climate change. So in order to get the change we need, our hearts must first change, then we will begin to have improved temperatures.

The focus should be to address the things that will have positive effects on the climate. Don't waste billions of dollars on the wrong kind of education, while we neglect to address the real issues.

Theological education to show the connection between the scientific and the theological. The very word which describes one of the three characteristics of God Himself is the term "Omniscience" from which comes the word "Science".

In order to change our environment physically and spiritually, we need to:

1. Put Family first and keep family as first priority overall

2. Build low-income houses and bring an end to squatting.

3. Give Grants and loans to improve the welfare of the poor, particularly in the rural areas.

4. Set up Prayer Centers throughout the country.

5. Promote Wholeness not Wellness

6. Consistently declare God's Word. The world was created with words and only the word can bring healing to the climate.

7. Constantly play Christian music which praises the Creator and not the creation

8. Train Rivers and cease building in water shed and flood prone areas

9. Establish new wells

10. Significantly increase the use of Solar Panels for Solar Energy to cut down the use of nuclear-powered energy, and include free solar panel donations in various communities.

11. Cease interference with the population through population control.

12. Cease certain scientific testing on the atmosphere which are now backfiring

13. Ban some of the fertilizers being used in our soil and get back to basics – organic.

14. Test all fish for nuclear contamination.

15. Have a massive tree-planting drive in every community – involve the schools and businesses.

Climate Change and God

"You alone are the Lord; you have made heaven, the heaven of heavens, with all their host, the earth and everything on it, the seas and all that is in them, and you preserve them all. The host of heaven worships you." (Nehemiah 9: 6)

As we read this Scripture, we (as well as the 150 countries that gathered in Paris recently), must realize that there can be no debate or discussion on climate change without including God.

The meetings were held in an effort to find a workable plan to stave off global catastrophe. When we change – when mankind chooses to change their way of thinking and of operating, then we will not have to worry about climate change.

Before the fall of man, the original order of man's environment on earth must be distinguished from what it became following the impact of man's fall. The curse and the eventual deluge; the agricultural, zoological, geological and meteorological disharmony to which creation has been subjected, must not be attributed to God who gave us a perfect earth. It is man's sin that has brought about what man refers to as climate change.

Global leaders who want to have a serious discussion about and find solutions to climate change, must have the Bible as a guide, going all the way back to Genesis to see how man's actions affect the globe.

Climate change does not only affect mankind. It affects the earth, the environment, the animals and the sea. The rebellion of man against God and the push to have a godless society is a greater threat than climate change.

Man's rebellion in times past, brought about a great flood. It also caused a permanent change in weather activity called rain. Prior to rain, there was only mist and dew. Furthermore, the appearance of the rainbow is a symbol that God will not destroy the entire earth again by flood. (Genesis 9: 11 – 13; Genesis 8: 22)

The Solution Is Jesus

Isaiah 24: 5 – 6 clearly outlines what things can defile the earth and cause climate change. It speaks about violating spiritual laws which can bring defilement within the earth – including rebellion against God, war, injustice, breaking God's covenant, negative speech, perverted and defiling movies and music, legislating God out of schools, politics, government. Then you will begin to see floods, landslides, heatwaves, earthquakes and the rivers either drying up or taking back their old courses.

Eye, ear and skin diseases will resurface and worsen. (Jeremiah 2: 17) Man's ways defile the very economy of a nation. It stops growth and prosperity.

Mismanagement and unfair distribution of the earth's resources – gold, silver and so on – through greed, as well as the mistreatment of the poor, all contribute to climate change significantly and this is what they should be discussing and making active efforts to change.

Believe it or not, even our very negative words affect and can destroy the earth. (Hebrews 11; Proverbs 18: 22)

Greed

Trees are being cut down unnecessarily. The reef is being disrupted, unnecessary dredging is taking place, all under the guise of economic development. Many countries are ignoring

regulations which are affecting environmental safety. Toxic waste is continually being dumped into the sea. Nuclear weapons testing and other dangerous tests by world powers are now destroying our marine life.

Our seafood and sea water are no longer safe. If the minority continues to control the wealth and things continue as they are, then we will further destroy the very thing that God gave man to manage. (Genesis 1: 26; Genesis 2: 15)

The Bible is our God-given operational manual to manage earthly affairs. Everything is in it, including how to avoid certain catastrophes. Even our agriculture has suffered. Let us recognize that everything is connected; and as such, Leviticus 25: 3 – 5, reminds us that a day is given for man to rest, so even the earth must rest. There needs to be a global regulatory body to police scientists and developers as well as undersea activities including certain blasting and digging. So much is being destroyed under the banner of science and economic development – including valuable watershed areas. Some of the fertilizers are destroying the earth.

Many nations seek to remove what they view as religion from their grand plans regarding the environment. However, they must recognize that excluding God and His instructions regarding the management of the resources of which He has given us charge over, will come back to haunt us in no uncertain terms and we will all have to face it again if it is not resolved.

The Bible Reveals Cosmic Truths

It is critical for mankind to take note of Biblical predictions on cosmic issues. What will trigger some of these issues is mankind's interference with creation. Psalms 19: 3 outlines the material earth is the sphere in which heavenly messages operate. There is no limitation – all nations are embraced in this limitation. God speaks to every nation through His creation and once He speaks to us, we must acknowledge Him as Lord and Savior. This Scripture proves what many scientists have discovered; that the sun is enclosed in an envelope of fire. (Psalm 19: 4; Romans 1: 19 – 20)

There cannot be a creation without a creator. God's creation tells us about the power of the Creator. Thus, man has no excuse for not believing that a Creator exists – regardless of their profession or belief; whether a scientist or atheist.

David described the rotation of the earth from the viewpoint of man – that the sun revolves around the earth. By comparison, we use words like sunrise and sunset to describe earth's rotation, when technically, the sun does neither.

Nothing happens in the world without God revealing it to His people and to those who desire to listen. Even for scientists who are trying to prove that there is no God, all the signs are there before their eyes! We are about to see the Law of Four in the Cosmic events – Air, Land, Sea/River, Bird, Livestock.

In an effort to gain supremacy, some of man's actions such as nuclear testing, the development and use of dangerous chemicals, personal and private choices, and even the implementing of legislation to remove the Word of God from public forum, have served to facilitate the current Cosmic issues. This is the very same Word that reveals to us that God created the cosmos on the fourth day!

The Word of God, creates, forms and restores. The very economy that is in shambles globally has come about as a result of the absence of the Word in the Marketplace. When we replace it with negative, blasphemous words, it pollutes, defiles and creates the next threat – OZONE LAYER AND LUNAR PROBLEMS!

Joel 2 speaks about the Lunar eclipse, as well as Revelation 6: 12 and Acts 2: 20. We know that there is a Lunar eclipse scheduled for April 15 and October 8, 2014. What would happen if a cosmic problem results? Are we ready to handle that?

The Law of Four

Revelation 6: 7 – 8 speaks about the opening of the fourth seal. The Bible outlines that there will be widespread death on the earth! It further speaks about the voice of the fourth living creature and Pale Horse ridden by death which symbolizes disease and destruction resulting in innumerable deaths, and also speaks about it affecting a fourth (a quarter) of the earth.

Revelation 8: 12, "Then the fourth angel sounded: And a third of the sun was struck, a third of the moon, and a third of the stars, so that a third of them were darkened. A third of the day did not shine, and likewise the night."

Take note that the word 'eclipse' means 'the darkening of a heavenly body'

John was speaking about a cosmic convulsion, similar to the ninth plague that took place in Egypt – Exodus 10: 21.

So, we see lunar, solar and ozone problems. Furthermore, Luke 21: 25 says: "And there will be signs in the sun, in the moon, and in the stars; and on the earth distress of nations, with perplexity, the sea and the waves roaring"

Will we see a lot of skin diseases, heat waves, heat strokes, vision problems and even tsunamis, tidal waves, fires, earthquakes where there are no fault lines, and even inactive volcanoes erupting in places we didn't think they existed?

Are there already gases in the atmosphere that are causing illnesses to many but are unknown to scientists and they don't want to admit it?

Will there be unbearable heat around the world and will we see an increase in dryness of the mouth and throat especially among the youth and elderly? Is there enough medication for the resulting diseases?

Will we now reap the consequences of the pollution of the ocean – the vessels and waste matter sunken in it?

The scientists must stop interfering with God's creation under the guise of research which is now backfiring on us globally!

Will the sun begin to kill the livestock and other animal life?

What will happen to energy costs and how will the poor be able to handle that?

Why don't the various agencies come together globally and put a plan in place to being to store vaccines, drinking water, and other necessary items?

Chapter 3

SURVIVAL IN DISASTER

It is critical to understand Times and Seasons and what to do in a particular season. Preparation is the key for survival. It is not if we are going to have a disaster it is when. Haggai 1: 11 reveals to us that there will be drought upon the Land/Ground, Mountain, Grain, New Wine, Oil, Men, Livestock and the Labor of Your Hands.

Natural Disasters come in many ways and include floods, fires, tornadoes, earthquakes, volcanic eruptions, tidal waves, tsunamis, landslides, monsoons, hurricanes, cyclones and many other happenings. Not being properly prepared for survival in any of these circumstances can lead to death, starvation, riots and total economic collapse. When the state/nation gives bulletins, there is no in-depth information given on how to survive during and after the disaster, especially if it should come suddenly on us. For example, some will say that we are to have water, cash and food for up to 3 days for each person. But what happens to the poor who don't even have 1 meal per day? My point is, we need to know how to use the natural resources we have around us daily to save lives.

The Truth About Storms

Jonah 1: 4 – 5 says, "But the Lord sent out a great wind on the sea, and there was a mighty tempest on the sea, so that the ship was about to be broken up. Then the mariners were afraid; and every man cried out to his god, and threw the cargo that was in the ship into the sea, to lighten the load. But Jonah had gone down into the lowest parts of the ship, had lain down, and was fast asleep."

There are many debates about storms, hurricanes etc. According to the Webster's New College Dictionary, a "tempest" is "a violent storm with high winds, especially one accompanied by rain, hail or snow."

Storms come in many ways. There are storms of life that God speaks to us about in Psalm 46 and He lets us know that He is ever present in our time of trouble. We have storms to test the measure of our faith and Jesus said in the Scriptures "O ye of little faith..."

Storms cleanse the earth, purge, removes old things and brings new things to the forefront. It uproots trees and even blows seeds to new places. Storms can even create jobs for the poor. Storms reveal the hearts of those in leadership and whether or not they truly care for the people and are willing to offer assistance in times of disaster.

There are contrary winds which oppose God's will for your life. We see it in the Scriptures when the disciples were crossing over and there were contrary winds that Jesus rebuked.

In Matthew 14: 22 – 33 Jesus knew that the contrary wind was coming and furthermore He wanted to see if they were ready to go to the next level in the supernatural. He also wanted to show His humanity and reveal His Deity and power over the elements which He created. (Read Luke 8: 35; Mark 4: 39)

Storms also promote some and bring others to repentance. There are many Scriptures which tell us that God rides on the very wind. God speaks through nature and each person may receive a different message. Storms change priorities, mandates and motives. Storms also speak to us about apocalyptic happenings and things to come. (Luke 21; Revelation 6 – which are coming).

So, each person has a message; but what stood out to me is Jonah 1: 4 where God sent a great wind on the sea – a mighty tempest. This could have been what we would today call category 5 hurricane, because it threatened to break up a ship. This came about because of Jonah's disobedience because Jonah was running from the presence of God. He did not want to go and preach repentance to the people to whom God wanted to show mercy. So now, the question is, could it be that storms are coming up because of the disobedience of some of God's people who no longer want to preach repentance and have gone in a different direction doing their own thing? In the midst of all that Jonah was fast asleep in the midst of the boatful of people worshipping other gods. Jonah didn't even want to identify himself as a prophet of God until his life was threatened and he had no choice. Is that what it will take for the prophets of God to do what God says? In all of it, Jonah asked to be thrown overboard because He knew that it was him and his disobedience that brought on the storm. It is after that we see the transformation take place with those aboard the ship. So the Holy Spirit said to me – the storm preached the gospel that Jonah would not! So when men in different nations throughout the globe stop preaching the gospel and compromise, He will use nature to preach just as in the days of Noah. And it will not just threaten the lives of the saved but also the unsaved. We will see many disasters globally unless we preach the gospel.

Those governments and organizations who refuse to change direction and refuse to help the poor the fatherless and the widow, and refuse to embrace Godly environment and principles will end up 'shipwrecked' and will spend far more than they bargained for to recover from natural disasters.

When we fail to listen to God's true servants, then we will have to listen to the wind and nature that don't need permission, regulations or visas and cannot be sanctioned, regulated or zoned.

Things To Know

1. The Styrofoam that we get in boxes and even the disposable plates, cups and other such containers can be used to make floating devices by tying them in a plastic bag or backpack and that can become your personal floating device in a flood.

2. You can also use any pants as a floating device by tying the foot of the pants together and flap it to get air in it and then tying the waist. While it is not as easy to do as other things, nothing beats trying.

3. Minimizing the use of plastic in our society today is not a bad idea, but it is the wrong timing to do this, because we are going to need all these plastic items for safety and security in times of disaster. The plastic is not the major part of the problem; it is our discipline disposing of the plastic items.

4. Tree stumps can be kept instead of destroying them, because both tree stumps and logs float in the water.

5. Always have a flashlight and a few batteries at the ready.

6. Always have your things in order in one place in case you have to beat a hasty retreat. For example, your shoes, your keys, your medication, a packed bag/suitcase, your dentures and any other personal items should be close together so it is easier to grab and go.

7. Never forget, when danger comes, listen to the still small voice – the Holy Spirit; and never forget Psalm 91 and Psalm 121 as well as Jeremiah 33: 3. Call upon His name – it works!

8. In a fire, the key thing is to have a wet towel or wet clothes over your nose to protect your lungs from the smoke. The smoke is more dangerous than the fire itself. Also, stay close to the ground. Don't run through a door, because you don't know what is happening on the other side.

9. Have all your important papers in one place at all times, and if possible in a fireproof container.

Things To Have At All Times

Bleach, Lime Juice, Baking Soda, Salt, Honey, Skim Milk Powder, Canned Goods, Rope, Water Filter (If no filter keep sand and a large enough piece of white cloth to strain the water). Also, have shovels to dig as well as matches and lighters.

General Information

1. Boil the water for 3 minutes and add 6 drops of chlorine bleach per gallon of water and wait for 30 minutes before drinking.

2. To preserve meat, salt it and smoke it by placing it over a low fire.

3. Where you don't have cash, try the barter system. Offer to give something in exchange for what you need.

4. In case of Tsunami, head for higher ground. If you are in traffic, abandon the car and run.

5. You can also make your own baby wipes by using almond oil, olive oil, soap and warm water.

Remember too that honey, apple cider vinegar, cornstarch, peanuts, granola and crackers cannot be spoiled.

In an earthquake, head for open spaces if your building is not safe and you don't have refuge within.

Knowledge is power.

Chapter 4

WORLD POLLUTION – THE NEXT THREAT!

Based on past reports given by the World Health Organization (WHO), 3 million people die each year from the effects of air pollution alone. Furthermore, according to a WHO article, "According to Global Health Risks: Mortality and burden of disease attributable to selected major risks indoor air pollution is responsible for 2.7% of the global burden of disease."

With gold mining, nuclear waste, and contaminated ground water; coupled with uranium mining, acid rain and growing garbage heaps around the world, what will be the result when they all connect. Further to this, there have been numerous disasters in various parts of the globe, earthquakes, floods and oil spills and they are all affecting air, land and sea. Is the world really prepared for and outbreak? In addition to all this, add the nuclear weaponry testing that is taking place in certain parts of the world. Pollution affects the entire environment – air, land and sea.

Further to all this, while China is the world's fastest growing economy, it has the highest annual incidence of premature deaths triggered by air pollution in the world, according to a new study. The WHO report estimates that diseases triggered by indoor and outdoor air pollution kill 656,000 Chinese citizens each year, and polluted drinking water kills another 95,600.

Air Quality Advisor at the WHO Regional Office for Europe says "Air pollution is estimated to cause approximately two million premature deaths worldwide per year."

The Sea

Is marine life safe? The millions of life forms below the sea each have their function and provide a delicate balance necessary for every one of them to exist.

Is fish safe for human consumption? Most of the smaller nations don't have the high technology equipment to test for poisonous substances in the fish they cash and some of the fishes caught go directly from the nets to the household tables!

Cancers and unknown illnesses are going to come from consumption of contaminated sea food. What about skin cancers and other skin related diseases. Furthermore, every person who enters the sea directly ingests some of its water.

What about internal problems? When man tries to circumvent God's laws, even concerning nature, suffering increases and even the very grass will wither and die. Diseases that we have never seen before will arise and it is the responsibility of every leader to have a pollution-free environment.

The Land

The issues that arise concerning land will undoubtedly affect our drinking water, ground water and the entire agricultural sector. Our livestock will be affected and human life in general because we all live on land.

Further to this, if human beings consume the meat from livestock and they are infected because of the water they drink, human beings will contract the diseases as well, and it may even worsen in humans.

The Air

Polluted air will cause serious respiratory diseases, skin diseases, diseases affecting the eyes and ear infections. The lungs will be most affected by these problems.

Solutions

1. All the nations need to come together and invest heavily in Environment-Friendly Activities because pollution will be the greatest threat ahead. There has to be monitoring and testing done in all countries to see what each nation's greatest threat is and how to alleviate it.

2. There needs to be major national clean-ups globally and the First world nations must necessarily invest in smaller countries, because all nations are connected environmentally.

3. A major storage of vaccines, respiratory masks, respiratory medications, eye-drops and medication, sanitizes, water purification tablets and machinery and garbage collection receptacles must take place.

4. Garbage dumps need to be moved from urban areas.

5. More tanks need to be built to cultivate fresh fish in order to sustain good health.

6. There needs to be more solar powered cars or vehicles that use an alternative to petrol.

7. Give more training in schools at all levels – from primary to tertiary – on dealing with environmental issues and hazards.

8. Protect and secure the water catchment areas and tanks.

9. Most leaders are ignoring environmental problems for investment, but there needs to be a balance, otherwise, it will be useless to invest and not live to enjoy it!

10. More countries need to go green! We must go back to being GREEN!

11. More needs to be spent on the Public Health Sectors to monitor certain sectors.

12. Four main areas of concern must be addressed – the air, the water, the sea life and the bird life, before disease and death skyrockets. God gave us the world free from pollution and we need to fix and maintain it as far as possible.

Water Shortage: The Next Crisis

Water is life – a commodity which is difficult for man to survive without. I believe that the value of water is even more than that of gold and diamonds, and that this will be undoubtedly evident in the future. The issue of water is number six of the 17 United Nations Sustainable Development Goals.

The World Bank and the United Nations are sounding the alarm about a global water -crisis ahead. The report, based on two years of research, says that 700 million people are at risk of being displaced by intense water scarcity by 2030. More than two billion -people are -compelled to drink unsafe water, and more than

4.5 billion people do not have safely -managed sanitation services.

There is a crisis brewing and most of the world's leaders are putting this issue on the backburner. Many are focused on crime and the economy without realizing that water is life! Without proper planning and preparation, this pending water crisis can trigger absolute disaster; and I know that should this happen, many would blame climate change.

There is a lot of water worldwide, but not much of it is drinkable. With all the pollution that exists in our world today, in addition to the floods happening worldwide, millions living in the river basins, people carrying out building and infrastructural expansions across the board, we are looking at a water crisis in the eyes. Most countries, particularly in the Caribbean, have not done much to upgrade, improve or expand their water-processing systems, plants and technologies, and they have not developed their wells and springs. Most are spending more time working on their roads, building new roads, expanding security, and so on. In the very near future, it is the countries who have water that will have power.

Water is mentioned in the Bible more than any other material/resources (Genesis 21: 14-15). David, Jeremiah and Jesus all told us the importance of water, physically and spiritually. Water existed before the earth, as we came to know it, was formed, and the entire economic foundation of earth was created out of water, even before man was formed. This should give us an idea of how important water is to the existence of every living thing on this planet. We all depend on water. It also carries the symbol of -abundance, blessing, the Holy Spirit, cleansing, purification and the Word (of God).

In the Bible, water shortage would be deemed as a curse. Further, the scriptures in 2 Kings 2: 19, shows us that a city can be in a good place but without water, the land will be unproductive. Archaeologists have determined that a good spring and good quality of water were the determining factors of where someone would settle.

Water was so important that the commodity and its sources were highly guarded. They knew that if the enemy was going to sabotage a nation, they would attack their water system. That being said, what do you think could potentially happen to the 'land of wood and water'?

I wouldn't be surprised if the next world war started over water, because conflicts and wars have occurred in the past between - neighboring nations (Genesis 26).

God's Displeasure

In biblical days, water was important to both ancient Israel and Palestine – essential for the daily needs as well as agricultural pursuits. Drought and famine would cause the people of God to come unto Him. God would use water as an indication of His displeasure with, or judgment of, His people. The drought and the dying of the livestock would bring the people back to God.

It is critical for the Caribbean and Latin American nations and all Third-World nations to begin putting plans in place, and they must be careful not to be persuaded by any nation or international lenders to divest their water. Instead, they should begin to put a team in place who are critical thinkers to identify springs, dormant wells, a good water table, and put plans in place for safeguarding and developing such areas, with a view to sustain the nation and exporting this invaluable resource.

There also needs to be a flat-rate meter -system in place for the poor.

Chapter 5

FLOOD, FAMINE, FOOD AND WATER

Disasters have been afflicting nations worldwide and, without a doubt, have been creating a serious, negative impact on the national and world economies. As a result, growth and development have been involuntarily sidelined in order for government to maintain a grip on things while attempting to repair the damage – physically and otherwise.

Without a doubt, we have entered a new path and a new era. We are now seeing nature speaking to mankind. For years, we have been outlining that there needs to be a plan, both individually and nationally.

From time to time, particular Third-World countries wait until there is a threat to put a temporary plan in place, and after the threat has passed, they go back to square one. If countries are going to become viable and survive, then we have to change the way we think as well as our modus operandi.

Very shortly, different countries will only be focusing on their own welfare – because every nation will be affected by a disaster of some kind. Third-World countries are often looking to other nations for assistance, and that is a mistake. Flood, famine, food and water will be the focus of every nation and it is critical for Jamaica and other Caribbean and Third-World countries to have an excellent contingency plan – particularly since the water in this region is of such high quality. Water will be gold in a time to come, and the recent hurricanes have already proven that. During the hurricanes, there was a shortage of water and the price of water increased significantly. In fact, there were some instances that the price of water per case was 10 times the original price. So water that sold for US$3.99 per case was being sold for $39.99 per case. Some states had severe water shortage.

Emergency Plans

It is critical that different heads of states begin to work along with UN bodies – especially the FAO (Food and Agriculture Organization), UNEP (United Nations Environment Programme), WFP (World Food Program), UNDRR (United Nations Office of Disaster Risk Reduction – formerly the UNISDR), UNHCR (United Nations Commissioner of Refugees), WHO (World Health Organization), UNV (United Nations Volunteers) – to put effective and proper emergency and response plans in place to save lives. Many countries may think they are safe and that they don't face what another region does. But, natural disasters can happen anywhere and nothing can stop them. They don't need a visa, they don't adhere to regulations, and they don't need permission to occur in a particular place. The nations need to have permanent and mandatory evacuation plans for all those who live in flood-prone areas and those who live close to the ocean or sea. Our seas and oceans are no longer safe and nations are now prone to tsunamis, tidal waves, monsoons, cyclones, typhoons, earthquakes and volcanic eruptions under the seas. This is not just about apocalyptic happenings as we find in Luke 21; but scientists and many countries have been interfering with and testing various weapons and actions in the seas and other areas in our environment which itself has a delicate balance, and now things have become dangerous. Marine life is now threatened and many countries, for the sake of economic development, has interfered with our environment, building in areas they should not.

Nations Now Need To:

1. Identify the old riverbeds and courses that have been 'developed' and built on and pull out of those areas. There needs to be intensive 'river training' activities and building of protective walls. More dams need to be built. Food storage must be implemented at both individual and

national levels to prevent price gouging, which will lead to famine and starvation.

2. Coordinate with churches and other non-governmental organizations to provide support to deal with the spiritual needs of the people. Oftentimes, there is great focus on providing food and other physical amenities, but no attention is given to the mental and emotional toll that disasters have on individuals and as a result, that aspect is neglected.

Serious problems with weather patterns will continue. Tsunamis, earthquakes, flooding, fire, and hailstones will occur. Most geographical areas and landscapes will change. Environmental problems will increase. Food and water will be contaminated because of the high level of activities within the ocean. The fish are not safe, and there needs to be major testing.

There is good and bad that can be found in the midst of a famine, however. Nations and organizations that are properly prepared always have an advantage and will have dominion in times of famine. Stockpiling and logistics are key in moving forward. The question then becomes: Is there enough food, medication or water available globally to deal with a global famine?

Chapter 6

POVERTY

What Brings Us Into Poverty?

Lack of knowledge and wisdom, debt, spending more than we are making or receiving, non-tithers, not helping the poor, lack of multiple incomes, generational curse, lack of vision, disobedience to God, witchcraft and sin, unfair distribution of resources in the wrong hands, regulatory and government agencies who allow certain persons certain opportunities (red tape/bureaucracy - where the normal man cannot get into certain places). Also, high taxation, wrong choices, undermining and sabotage, unforgiveness, wrong mindset, lack of faith, lack of cash flow to purchase assets. Know this, the rich don't use their money at times to purchase, they use our money.

The question is what are we willing to cut in order to come out of debt that we can begin to have some form of saving? A higher paying job without the knowledge and wisdom will not allow you to be financially better, higher job, higher tax. So, if your habit remains the same, you will always be struggling.

There are many things we can start to cut to become financially better and change our climate. We can begin to cut back on the amount of food we consume on a daily basis, cut down the wastage, cut out the sugary drinks and use lime and lemon water, cut some unnecessary bills within our house. We must begin to learn about saving and investment, having money in the bank without interest makes no sense. We have to think like the rich. We go to school to manage, but the rich goes to own, we have to go for ownership. So, the key to come out of poverty is our mindset first has to change.

Our Approach To Poverty

Never agree with poverty, God wants us to prosper according to 2 John 3. You have to take authority over poverty, begin to speak, there are miracles in your mouth. Do not embrace poverty. Ask the Holy Spirit to fill you and open your eyes to the truth that he will show you and the things that he has in store for you. 1 Corinthians 2:9 and John 10:10,

Deuteronomy 28: 11 – 13 specifically speaks to us of things God wants to bless us with. We don't have to embrace lack, limitations and cycles. God gives us several things to change our environment, prayer, fasting, decree and declare, giving, all of these change your environment.

The Holy Spirit, wants to break bareness from our lives, we must break barrenness and loose the spirit of grace and abundance. Everything I touch shall be fruitful, begin to declare it both physical and spiritual. (2 Kings 2:19-22)

Barrenness attacks prosperity, whether it is barrenness of the womb, instability, a barren land, lack of ideas. Barrenness brings the spirit of poverty, poverty is a spirit. Most times that spirit will try to attack you because of your purpose. It may be coming from a generation or the community you reside. Jesus had to pull a man out of a community to bring change to him. Your environment can impact your sight and your vision, even people around you, God wants to restore us, but sometimes he has to pull us from people and even familiar places to open our eyes. Poverty limits our access and our influence. It brings depression, hopelessness, burden and helplessness. Prayer breaks poverty and barrenness. (Isaiah 65: 23 – 25)

We must call upon the Lord, just as He commanded the ravens to feed Elijah, He will command human ravens to also feed you. When God commands no one can stop it. We must understand that it is not Baal who controls the weather and the prosperity, it is God who controls it. Even in drought, the prophet was never under the jurisdiction of Baal, he was under the jurisdiction of God and that is why God fed him even in famine and he will feed you too. God will use any source to bless his people, even people you may consider unclean, to bring food to bless his people, so we should never look down on anyone in society because we will never know the source of our blessing, where it will come from. It is time for us to begin to push back from barrenness and poverty.

Ask the Lord to give you a millionaire mind, find scriptures with abundance and blessing and provision and begin to declare it. Open your mouth and speak because the enemy is also speaking against you. We must attack this spirit, because this spirit even attacks those who God instructs to bless you for them not to obey when God speaks to them to bless you. There is no shortage of resources in heaven or on the earth, we have a distribution problem and a spirit of poverty that wants to limit the Kingdom people from advancing and that is why we need to ask the lord to command the blessing, those God speaks to bless us, needs to obey and give up when God instructs them to give to us. That they themselves can be blessed.

Chapter 7

POVERTY AND CLIMATE CHANGE

Poverty carries a climate – crime, hopelessness, sickness, bondage, oppression and dominion of those who have control the wealth in certain communities. Very rarely will you see, for example, an abortion clinic in a place of prosperity.

Over seventeen (17) years ago, world leaders in assessing the global landscape, agreed on the Millennium Development Goals (MDGs): a set of time-bound and quantified targets for addressing the many dimensions of extreme poverty, including hunger, disease, lack of adequate shelter, and exclusion; while promoting gender equality, education, and environmental sustainability. When the MDGs were agreed, there was a general acknowledgement of the fact that social development is a key component of the sustainable development of the whole human race. It works in tandem with economic, political and other forms of development.

Regrettably, in the intervening years, uneven and unequal global development meant that although some progress was made, many countries, particularly developing ones, failed to meet some of the MDGs. Today, more than 1 billion people still live in extreme poverty. They continue to struggle with limited access to basic services, including education, health services, safe drinking water and sanitation. Rising inequality and exclusion, unemployment and lack of decent work opportunities also remain problems in many countries. These unattained, social dimensions of development comprise much of the "unfinished business" of the MDGs that led to the calls for a new global paradigm to succeed them.

Today, there are more national disasters happening globally, and as I have said in previous articles, poverty and climate change and the new wave of natural disasters occurring are urgent issues on which we need to focus and act.

Most countries don't remember the agreement they made when they all came together in 2000. They are no longer living up to their promises and responsibilities. The drastic measures now being put in place – cutting benefits to the people, implementing stringent laws and practices that hurt rather than help them, are now negatively affecting the peoples of the nations to the detriment of their country.

For example, the 2017 Hurricane Season is the costliest in history up to this point, racking up damages totaling

US$370 billion worldwide, with over US$200 billion in damages occurring in the United States of America. The question is, if the natural disasters continue on their current trend, and even affect those areas where oil is being drilled, for example, then how will we all be affected? Will oil prices skyrocket? Will we be able to afford petrol? How will that affect public transportation costs?

As things stand, over 783 million people are living below the international poverty line of US$1.90 per day. How will a continuation of these disasters affect that situation? What contingency plans do governments globally have for these occurrences?

3 out of every 10 persons lack access to safely managed drinking water and 6 out of every 10 people lack access to safely managed sanitation facilities. Should the disasters continue, how do they impact this situation?

The Current Economic Climate

Poverty hinders true potential plus it denies the generation or individual to get access to certain areas in the society. Now you know why just one type of person will dominate or given access to certain sector plus the political arena. It hinders also the advancement of Kingdom dominion. When one is in poverty, they will never have access to certain places, people, or certain offices within society unless god gives you favor like Joseph and Daniel in the Bible.

Solutions and Priority Shifts

We have a crisis, and Governments, Businesses and Civil Society now must come together and change their focus. They must begin to focus more on the poor. Many talk about cyber security and this digital era, meanwhile people are not just suffering but are dying as a result of neglect. Cyber, digital and all that will mean nothing when someone is sick and hungry.

Nations need to actively engage in intensive food security programs at both national and individual levels. This extends to protecting marine life, including fish stocks which, given environmental and other threats to the oceans, means the world food supply will diminish even further as world population grows and more natural disasters take place.

Give more support for farming, not only in promoting it as a viable means of income Farming – those in poverty-stricken nations have a low-scale farming. So, training is needed for them to improve their farming methods and output. Thus, productivity will increase and a market can be established for the produce.

Support the development of micro-industries such as plant nurseries to grow flowers; or water purification plants to produce water for sale, thereby creating employment.

Make warehouse space available for storage of basic items.

Remove tax and customs duties from food items, water, tents and certain basic medical equipment and farmers' tools.

Governments must work with NGOs and Churches to coordinate plans for assistance. There also needs to be more training on issue fueling poverty as well as a harnessing of ideas from the people of the nation.

Chapter 8

THE GLOBE MUST HAVE A PLAN

Everything under the sun has a season. The Good Book teaches us about Times and Seasons. We may not be able to stop what each season may bring, but we can capitalize on each season and become rich, minimize loss and save lives. No investor wants to make a loss, but if we fail to plan, then plan to fail.

During the last recession, because many did not plan, many investors were blown out of the market and numerous Christians lost their assets in the real estate meltdown.

Planning is simply thinking ahead on paper and your plans must focus on the seasons ahead. So, we must then ask the question: "What is most critical for our survival ahead?"

Critical Survival Recommendations

As an answer to the question, most countries may think the focus should be gender and/or climate issues. However, food and water are the most critical things for survival. We should learn from Pharaoh and Joseph in the Bible, who created long term agricultural policies and infrastructure for the nation's survival. (Genesis: 41: 46 – 57)

It is critical for us to understand and accept that we have no control over Acts of God nor certain man-made problems. However, if we have a plan/vision, we can weather any storm and remain profitable.

Leaders Must Know Times and Seasons

Many are talking about the cyber/digital revolution; but what plans are in place if there is a blackout? Have we not seen Facebook, Twitter and Instagram crash and Venezuela experience a nationwide blackout? And while the different countries blame and accuse each other of sabotage, what if this becomes the new norm – country against country – what plans do we have in place?

In the same way that many leaders are excited about the latest software/gadget/technology and are enticed to upgrade to the latest version, it is critical for leaders to upgrade spiritually in order to remain relevant and be an effective leader. To be a transformational leader, you yourself must first be transformed by renewing your mind. You must think and look beyond academics in order to solve the problems ahead.

Economics

The world is a small place, what happens in one place can impact several other regions and national economies. For example, the plane crash in Ethiopia recently has impacted every nation in the globe and has the potential to cause economic fallout in some nations as these nations are now banning that particular air craft model.

Every economy needs to be built on the Solid Rock – not on the sand of our own logic and human know-how.

Every Head of State, every national Treasurer, and Agricultural Minister will be tested to see the quality of their nation's economic foundation. Whether they want to hear about it or not, there must be research on Apocalyptic events/happenings and the results applied to their decision-making. For example, the symbolism of the White, Red, Black and Pale horses. The increase of diseases and disasters will put greater pressure on nations' economies. Are we prepared for that?

Further, with the World Bank President – Jim Yong Kim – jumping ship, will we see a new culture coming out of the World Bank where it is no longer easier for poorer countries to receive financial assistance and ultimately cause a shift from cash to card, forcing other nations to print larger currencies?   Are we prepared for that?

Here's A Plan

Investors and governments must begin to invest in land, food, bauxite, warehouses, as well as the health and pharmaceutical industries. They need also to invest in tanks, water, emergency supplies and other items for survival. Farming should also be the number one priority. Planting fruit trees and vegetables and cultivating fresh water fish.   They should also be building hospitals and veterinary clinics. We need to build more bakeries.

Furthermore, the banks have the opportunity at this time to reduce interest rates and lend to farmers to purchase irrigation systems, solar panels, and equipment for food preservation to allow for stockpiling and storage.

Government can begin to reduce General Consumption Tax and Sales Tax and remove tax from all farming items including seeds.

There must also be plans in place for transportation, logistics and storage to deal with possible economic crises if there is a fallout.

The writing is on the wall. We must have a plan.

Time For a Detox

We are living in a society where almost everything we take in is fake. There are fake foods, fake water, fake hair, fake body parts and even fake news. We are living in a toxic environment which is highly polluted. There is even pollution and high toxicity within the Body of Christ and only the undiluted, 100% organic Word of God can cleanse us.

Health practitioners will say it is good to detox ourselves regularly. Physically, we can use lemon juice, vinegar and a lot of water. We can eat our meals where 50% of what is on our plates is cooked and the other 50% is raw/uncooked (raw vegetables). A toxic body causes illness because it means we are filled with waste matter that needs to come out and it slows us down and causes many illnesses.

There are so many things in our society that needs to be detoxed from our systems. For example, negative people, gambling, sexual impurities, adultery, fornication and gossip. When God calls us from darkness to light, the first thing He does is to detox us by allowing the things or the people who are not healthy for us to be removed – a purging – which is a form of detoxing. He removes the weight and the filth that has bogged us down over the years. Sadly, we often fight to hold on to those people and things, including circles, groups, companions and even organizations. But we have to realize and embrace the fact that Jesus is trying to make us healthy – body, soul and spirit. He wants us to be clean. (Hebrews 10: 2) Oftentimes, the problems we are encountering are a significant part of our detox process. It may be painful, but as soon as the garbage and filth leave, we will begin to realize our true size and see who we really are. Our joy will begin to return. Purity is the key to prosperity

Have you ever felt full and bloated, heavy and stressed? You need a detox spiritually and physically. The old things must go. Everything is connected – body, soul and spirit. Many people will say they are healthy because they go to the gym and they do yoga and they take supplements. But what happens when they do all that and still harbor unforgiveness, hatred, jealousy, bitterness, or engage in sexual immorality and impurities? All those are toxins as well which impact the body and the soul. What about someone who does all that but has low self-esteem, negative thoughts and a bad attitude?

Detoxing the Environment

Detox is necessary even for the earth – oceans, rivers, and even the ground. Oftentimes when we see disasters - tsunamis and tidal waves, but it is a detox process that oceans are going through. The waste, toxins and debris that have been left in the oceans – whether by man's carelessness, or through man's rituals must come out. Even when flooding takes place, it's a detoxing that is taking place and all the garbage becomes exposed for removal. Could it be that even when the volcanos erupt, that there is a detoxing taking place below the surface.

So when man's actions, go against God's creation, then the earth, the environment becomes toxic and a purging/detoxing becomes necessary. Man has a great deal of influence on the state of the environment, so man's negative actions determine the reaction of the earth. So if all individuals and sovereign nations begin to detox the waste and poison corrupting us and the world, then we will not have to worry about climate change.

It is sad to say that the very things that were created to detox us is what is being destroyed and replaced with the fake.

Sweet But Sour

Sugar is sweet, but today sugar is poisoning our bodies. Sex is sweet, but when we go beyond the boundaries God set for it, then the whole body becomes toxic and defiled.

The very organs of the body were made to worship God. In the same way that the planetary bodies in the universe were created to do the same. (Psalm 148) it becomes an idol, and where the creation takes precedence over the creator, then it is time for a detox.

Chapter 9

FAMINE AND NATION-BUILDING

The success of every nation is determined by what they used to build the nation. King Solomon's success resulted from the fact that he did not just focus on building his house – the central government – but also focused on building God's house.

It is not just a physical house, but the establishment of laws that glorified God (1 Kings 9: 10). The building of God's house is never secondary, and the economy of a nation should never affect the building of God's house. Different nations have been building, but on what are they building? With what specifications are they building? Furthermore, to whom are they building? Which house are they building?

Building has to do with policies, laws, implementation methods, philosophies – similar to what we see in Genesis 11, where they wanted to build a global economic system without God's input or involvement. They were building God out of their plans and systems. They wanted the blessings of God without God. As a result, it brought chaos and downfall, famine, starvation, global migration and brain drain.

When we build God's house, He will build our house. Solomon understood and that is why he surpassed all the kings of the earth during his time, in riches and wealth (1 Kings 12: 24).

Abortion and Nation-Building

Recently, we saw a law being passed in New York to legalize the abortion of babies even up to full term, and the Trade Centre was lit up in celebration. That is building as well, but building to what and with what? And what will the reward be? Abortion does not happen in a vacuum. It is also the abortion of futures, nations and economies as well, and brings famine. So many Third-World nations – including Jamaica – are utilizing this building principle to build their country. Are they willing to deal with the consequences of that? They need to remember that the Chairman – the Sovereign, Supreme One – have both veto power and the power to override laws, treaties and resolutions (binding and non--binding). It is so disappointing to see young politicians simply abort their political future by supporting abortion to build nations.

Famine

Every person within each nation needs to know that the actions of past administrations affect present administrations. So even when new leaders are installed, they are often blamed for the misdirection of the nation caused by the actions of the past administrations. Recognize that unless there is atonement and restitution, the effects of the action do not simply disappear, and when harvest comes, then those effects will produce famine.

The Oxford Dictionary defines **famine** as *"extreme scarcity of food; starvation"*. From a biblical perspective, famine always comes to get the people back to God. It also promotes the true leaders. We have famine where/when there is war, and when crime and violence is on the increase. Famine for food, caused by drought, and it triggers price increases and food shortage. It affects livestock and agriculture in general. There is also the famine that is the result of economic systems crashing – recession, foreclosures, receiverships and massive murders are the result. However, the most dangerous one happens when God goes silent on a nation.

Preparation and Planning

We are in a time now where planning, preparation, positioning and stockpiling are the keys for survival. Nobody wants to be in a situation where the money we have become so greedy for becomes valueless, or to get to the stage where someone would be willing to give away their livestock and land just to get bread and water for survival.

In a famine, those who have food will always have power. So, if food and water become the order of the day, what will become of the stock market and the money we fought so hard to hoard?

Famine will also level the economic field, where economic equality results and everyone will be on the same level financially.

Famine tests every individual's foundation and also the foundation used to build and reveal who the true advisers are and who are not.

My advice is that each person take up their responsibility to have a plan in place for themselves and their family for survival, because when the dust settles at the end of the day, it will be every man for himself and loyalty will be a rare thing. The highest bidder will win.

Chapter 10

CHANGE THE CLIMATE OF BANKRUPTCY

There are many going through hardships and facing problems from every direction. Many ask the question, 'Why am I going through all this?' We often go through problems but recognize that they pull out of us the hidden potential we did not realize was within us. We go through problems and testing, but these experiences can help to strengthen us, and allow us to help others.

Oftentimes, we don't even remember God and His goodness until we are going through times of great difficulty. Many going through difficulty are giving up, and some are even committing suicide. Regardless of how big your problem may seem, recognize that every problem has an expiration date.

Your date can be today!

When you are going through problems, always focus on the problems from which the Lord has already delivered you. They are no longer problems, but victories. Remember the goodness and grace of God Who brought you through those problems. If He has delivered you from the problems before, He will do it again.

Focus on Victory

Many times, the problems we go through are based on our purpose, our assignment and the vow(s) we have made. Sometimes, people become comfortable and don't remember where they are coming from and God is trying to get our attention. Just remember, when going through the problems, don't focus on the problem, instead focus on the victory. When we focus on the problem, the mountain becomes greater.

There is always a solution within the problems, and sometimes that solution is what will allow you to become greater. Speak to your problems daily. Speak positive words and outcomes. For example, thank God for the victory you anticipate. Always find scriptural basis to deal with the problem. So:

1. If it is a sickness you are facing, then declare Isaiah 53: 5.

2. If you are going through bankruptcy or serious financial woes, then declare Psalms 112.

3. If a door has been closed to you and you don't know how to proceed, then declare Isaiah 43: 16.

Make and spend time with God and tell Him about the problems. Problems are a sign that God wants to get your attention. We are often too busy trying to do everything to survive, when God says we should seek Him first.

Maintaining a relationship with God is the key to success. Most countries and organizations are now failing. They have nothing new to download or to offer because they are spiritually bankrupt.

Many times, we pray for promotion and blessing, but God wants depth. There are too many people in this world that have height without depth and that's why there is a great falling.

Remember as II Corinthians 4: 16-18 reminds us: "Therefore we do not lose heart. Even though our outward man is perishing, yet the inward man is being renewed day by day. For our light affliction, which is but for a moment, is working for us a far more exceeding and eternal weight of glory; while we do not look at the things which are seen, but at the things which are not seen. For the things which are seen are temporary, but the things which are not seen are eternal."

Better Will Come

All we are going through is temporary. Our mind is being renewed and our inner man is being strengthened. Many times, people say they can't live without another pay cheque; but they must remember that God is their first source, and God can allow you to live without a pay cheque and live better than before.

Problems are the gates for change. Job only realized who his true friends were in his time of great adversity. He was going through the problems, not because he was cursed, but because God was proving who was around him and who was with him.

One of people's biggest fears in life is to lose things – your job, friends, family, status and position. Sometimes, you don't even know who you really are until you lose something or someone close to you.

Remember, an eagle does not learn how to fly until the mother stirs up the nest, and forces it out. The unjust servant did not know how good a negotiator and sales person he was until the boss planned to fire him. Sometimes, a person never knows who their Boaz or Ruth is until they get kicked out or hurt in a relationship.

Do not commit suicide in the midst of the problem - it doesn't solve the problem. You are using a permanent action for a temporary problem. Walk through it, you will come out! Greater is always ahead of you.

Chapter 11

RECESSION BRINGS NEW OPPORTUNITIES

In the marketplace today, there is great fear of a pending recession and it is causing global anxiety attacks. Many are calling for the replacement of the dollar, as the reserve currency. Some say there is going to be worldwide economic collapse/recession.

Any economic system built without the principles of God will always be unstable. God has a principle and a blueprint for each nation must operate regarding how they are to operate. It does not make sense to debate which system is better – whether socialism or capitalism. Both are flawed and both have failed the people.

Best System of Government

Socialism is mainly focused on Secularism – a system without God – and God is replaced with the word "State". Psalm 127: 1 reminds us that, "Unless the Lord builds the house, they labor in vain who build it; Unless the Lord guards the city, the watchman stays awake in vain." Once God is removed from the society, it becomes a Godless society.

Capitalism has also failed because of greed and corruption, and we have seen more countries which are deemed Capitalist, fail to protect the poor. More laws are being passed to marginalize the poor. While capitalism supports private ownership – being free to work, trade and own land – we have seen over the years, some of the greatest transfers of wealth from the poor to the rich, including bailouts for the wealthy while the poor are forced to live on the streets.

All things being considered therefore, the best system of government and economy would then be the Theocratic system of government with One Who champions for the poor – God! He has a welfare system for the poor. It is called the Law of Gleaning, which would take care of the poor who have fallen on hard times. It supports self-reliance, debt freedom, debt forgiveness and restoration of property after a specified number of years. It also supports big businesses writing off the debts of smaller business, and the debts of poorer nations being written off by the wealthier ones. All this teaches us that riches and wealth are gifts given by God to be extended to others in need.

When we see Capitalist countries begin to remove systems that would benefit the poor, likewise, Socialist countries are removing anything that mentions God at any level, then we are certainly heading for a recession.

Theocracy also supports Private Ownership – where trade can take place and family is the first priority. It operates with Grace, Mercy and Compassion.

Prayer Breaks Recession

Prayer is not a word that many like to hear, particularly in connection with the economy, financial systems and technology.

However, it is interesting to note that prayer is the first wireless communication and has been around since the dawn of time. Furthermore, it has always been free and the only way it is ineffective is when it is not done with a pure heart.

Prayer involves Intercession, Thanksgiving and Petitioning. Petitioning is a formal application or entreaty to an authority. It is also a written action by a government signed by a number of people.

God is the Ultimate Authority and the Final Government. Imagine what would happen if all the stakeholders in a nation came together petitioning God to bring change within the nations and even the global economy, and that righteous governance come into effect; change would take place worldwide.

The day any government, prime minister, president or monarch ignores criticism and ridicule, and calls their nation to one day of prayer for the Lord to intervene in the affairs of the nation, we would be surprised to see the solutions and the change that would come forth.

There is always such a fight against prayer. But if prayer is such a bad thing, then why ask for it during times of adversity?

Take note that prayer is extremely effective, so much so that it can break recession, change the economy and bring spiritual and natural revival, growth and prosperity to a nation. (1 Kings 18; Joel 1-2)

Persistence in prayer deals with injustice, disaster, evil, poverty and war. (Luke 18:1-8)

The number one priority in church, nation or business must be prayer – then the nation would have peace. The first wall of defense in a nation must be prayer, not weaponry and the national security forces. Unless the Lord build the house we labor in vain! (Psalm 127:1-2)

When the wall of prayer breaks down within a nation the following will occur (Ezekiel 13:5, Ezekiel 22:30):

1. Family divisions

2. Internal and external security issues

3. Governmental problems.

4. False doctrines, false teachers and powerlessness in church.

5. Attraction of the wrong advisers to the government.

6. Lack of new ideas and investment

7. Shift in the motives of those in the media

8. Wrong kind of educators entering the education system.

When the wall of prayer is torn down, then we have famine, recession, violence, corruption, evil, and great poverty.

Recession and Opportunities

The righteous should never fear recession, it raises up new millionaires and gives nations new direction, new advisors and transfers wealth into the right hands.

Recession has the potential to:

1. Show Who is really in charge of the economy – and that it provides major opportunities and support for the poor.

2. Allows other nations that are willing to apply Biblical Principles to begin to rise in and to power. Those who have food and water.

3. Farming will become the number one priority. People will begin to create new opportunities for survival. For example, gold, land acquisition, real property and the rental business, and franchising will all be the focus instead of the stock market. Instead of the banks, more private entities will come to the fore to give people an alternative for loans at a lower interest rate.

4. Allow for less manipulation, and as a result, a new market environment will emerge, that will change the way business will be done.

5. The Barter System, may once again emerge.

6. Faith and Trust in God will be restored and nations and businesses will begin to pray again for solutions. A new breed of managers and leaders will emerge – those who will not depend

on their academic qualifications to bring success but will instead trust God to do sol

7. The Church will (also) get back to their core mandate of dealing with the total man. There will be a fair distribution and the haves will help the have nots – similar to the Acts Church, where those who have more than one will willingly give to those who have none. (Acts 2: 42; Acts 4: 32 – 37)

We should not fear recession, because it acts as a societal and national reset, bringing things back to basics for a fresher, fairer start.

Chapter 12

EMPOWERMENT FOR ECONOMIC GROWTH

There are many conversations taking place about economic growth. Some are not growing at the level or to the extent of expectations. There are even debates and comparisons made about other countries, such as, China or India regarding economic growth. With this observation made, I ask the question: If economic growth is taking place in these countries, why is there no growth for the poor at the bottom? No nation will experience true economic growth until the feet of the nation begin to receive growth also.

Analyzing Our Resources

We need to analyze the strengths and weaknesses of our economy if we truly want to achieve workable goals. Are our goals as a nation workable? Are we willing to put away "the book" and open our minds to begin to look at things differently and think outside the box? We have to look beyond price, demand and supply, wages, labor and capital. Many will quickly believe that these are what affect GDP (Gross

Domestic Product) and GNP (Gross National Product).

First and foremost, we cannot grow the economy by taking God out of the picture. Even if some nations are experiencing certain growth, it is just a matter of time before it all comes crashing down and we start having negative growth. God gives every nation all the necessary natural resources and human resources to make them rich. What we have are managerial and political problems.

Each country must first look at the natural resources that exist in their nation and community and empower the people accordingly, so that they can properly harness and manage the natural resources and achieve success. For example, Jamaica has fruits, herbs, spices, doctors, farmers, dancers, water, athletics, culinary skills, churches and music, to name a few.

Harness The Potential Within

Why is the nation investing more heavily in every other areas where the people would ultimately leave to pursue a career and/or promotion connected to their area of study? We cannot get the economic growth we need when the people cannot even afford to pay their school fees, neither will we be able to expand the security force.   We seem to be the only country whose people do not believe in their own abilities to succeed.   Every expert brought in to bring development and growth is a foreigner. That says that we **do not** believe in our own people. In most cases, the foreigners bring their brand of "first world" plans and strategies that are not even compatible with our people and our natural resources. We need to recognize that "First World" does not necessarily mean "Better World".

In order to achieve true economic growth, we need to move beyond setting everything up around a cash system. We will need to have a plan for the people and their empowerment – Individual Growth first. When people have Town Hall Meetings, instead of using it as a feeding ground to shove ideas and ideologies down the throats of the people, it should be used to present what they have and then listen to the solutions that the people come with for betterment also, with a willingness to implement those ideas from the people that can actually work.

Always remember that man's actions affect economic growth and development.   The environment we create is what we will get. Instead of talking about Climate Change, we should focus more on our actions, utilize whatever resources we have and build low income houses. Do more in the areas of Education and Community Empowerment.

The Spiritual Side of Growth

It is strange that people are focusing on Marxist theories for Economic Growth rather than utilizing the principles of the Bible. God created the economy even before He created man; Man messed it up. But since God created it, He can fix it too. Righteousness creates Economic Growth and Development. Seeking God first, leads us to Economic Growth. When we abide in Him (John 15) then He will begin to open our eyes to the gold within our midst. Hence, we will not have a situation similar to that of Africa where people went in and extracted the precious resources (gold, diamonds) without a care for the people or the continent's Economic Growth and Development.

God's word, prayer and fasting all lead to Economic Growth. Nothing will grow without these elements.

The Four P's For Growth

Everyone wants growth of some kind - whether Economic or Spiritual. But we cannot receive economic growth without spiritual growth, so both the spiritual and the natural are connected.

True growth starts with God. Isaiah 48: 17 says, "Thus says the Lord, your Redeemer, The Holy One of Israel:

"I am the Lord your God, Who teaches you to profit, Who leads you by the way you should go." Oftentimes people brag about their uncanny business sense or their wisdom in a situation that allowed them to succeed – without acknowledging Him – God.

The following P's are strategies to bring true growth, that is, so well needed in this time.

Prayer

Prayer is the key to receiving the Promises of God, and brings the fulfillment of God over our lives. Prayer brings power, keeps us pure, gives us spiritual, physical and emotional healing and also give us the access that every person needs – including businessmen, Prime Ministers and Presidents. Prayer breaks famine, opens the heavens for rain, breaks lack and poverty, changes our climate and our environment. It also brings economic cure. Prayer also brings boldness and solutions. Sadly, many times we pray, but we do not listen for the response from God. Prayer is a two-way communication activity - speaking and listening - and then act on what we are told.

Persistence

In Business or any other area of life, you will have opposition and struggles. There is nothing wrong with the world itself, the issue lies with the people. There are people within the world who feel they are entitled to all the wealth and access, so they always try to put stumbling blocks before others. This is why we have to be firm and persistent in times of difficulty. We must function with tenacity, endurance and determination are keys to growth. For every profit there is a loss, but it is important to press forward; there will be obstacles. Never yield, never give up! Keep wrestling with God. Ask, Seek, Knock. Doors of access will open and justice will be served. People who are denied justice, should keep pressing, as it was done in Luke 18: 1 – 10. Sometimes, the greater the failure, the greater the growth. Look at the stories of KFC and Disney and you will understand.

Preparation

Planning for the future is key to Preparation. If we are to experience growth, we have to plan for the future generation. The people of a nation must be prepared before growth can take place. This is one of the reasons education, particularly a good education, is of such vital importance to any nation.

Preparation brings great savings and allows us to capitalize on new opportunities. For example, if you are in the midst of a drought and there is no vessel prepared to store the water, then when the sudden burst of showers come, you will waste time trying to find vessels, meanwhile the precious resources will be wasted. Furthermore, all those waiting to benefit from those resources would suffer a loss.

Most countries do not prepare for the future, most of them simply try to do damage control when the time comes. Take note:

If Joseph was not prepared, he would not have been able to bring the solution for the economic downturn by storing food and planning distribution.

Noah had to prepare the ark for the flood.

The biggest hindrance to blessings is the lack of Preparation. We must also plan for battle in order to maintain growth. We must plan for famine and disasters, and we need to plan for blessings and expansion. God does not promote us unless we prepare. He, by example, always prepares the place before He brings us to it. For example, in marriage you will need to possess the qualities of a wife before He allows you to be one. Additionally, according to Genesis 1, the Lord prepared the earth before He put mankind in it.

Fasting, Prayer and Giving are also part of the Preparation process.

Promotion

Passion, Humility and Diligence come before Promotion.

Every person, every nation desires elevation in every area of their existence, including ratings. God always promotes us, whether physically, financially and brings greater access for greater growth when we obey Him. Growth/Increase is a part of Promotion.

Chapter 13

IMPORTANT WORLD SOLUTIONS

Disaster Solutions

Those with massive investments in the agricultural industry will suffer great losses as a result of the disasters and it will cause a massive shortage in food including, peanuts, potatoes and other vegetables. This will cause a major famine throughout the world. But the Lord says prophetically, "If My people who are called by my name will cry out, then I will show mercy, and My people will be fed during the famine. As they obey Me, worship Me and give their Tithe, they will be protected."

Pray for all places where oil is found and all places where the drilling is taking place, as there will be many disasters. Most of them will crash and workers will be running frantically. It will cause an oil shortage and increase the prices significantly.

For years there has been a call for strategic plans for storage of water and food. In Jamaica, the Caymanas area should not have been designated for building because of the necessary water storage and protection of the waters there. Water and food will be critical and we cannot continue to look at Climate Change from a singular perspective.

Economic Solutions

1. After taking one tenth of their earnings which is their Tithe, take out another tenth as savings in the event of an economic crash.

2. Revisit insurance policies for their businesses and increase those policies.

3. Stock cases of water, canned items and coal and basins.

4. Give what they can to their community, focus on the poor throughout the island. Set an urgent program which will provide poor families with basic necessities: Food, Water, Shelter, Clothing, and Money.

5. Assist with On-The-Job Training programs and Job Training programs externally which will open up doors to desired jobs.

6. Assist children in Tertiary Level Education Placement (Universities and Colleges).

7. High Schools, Universities and Colleges must have curricula with strong emphasis on Entrepreneurship and Job Creation.

8. Focus more on the **P.O.O.R.** – **P**overty-stricken **O**utcasts **O**utsiders and **R**ejects

9. Investment, Stocks and Bonds, Real Estate Companies, Media Houses, Art Galleries, Credit Unions, Law Firms, Restaurants, Financial Firms – God wants His people to invest in these areas.

Media Houses

Take to the streets more in every parish and change the way you, the media, see people.

Design a segment for the poor especially those living on the streets who are neglected by society and genuinely show empathy. Network with other organizations also – NGOs, Churches, etc. To donate items such as food, clean quality clothing: socks, shoes, blouses, skirts, dresses, underwear, sandals, building low income houses, visit schools nationwide to speak with children of all ages, asking the children what help they think the church and the government should give, visit various companies of all sizes and do free advertisements for them for at least a week.

Interview workers and clients/customers asking them what they think will help them more effectively as clients/customers and staff.

New Mind, New Wine New Business

To deal with the economic crises and other global social issues we are facing, as leaders we must always dig deeper each day in the things of God, in order to get the necessary solutions. Time changes, people change, the market demands change – EVERYTHING CHANGES! Even the rate of the dollar changes! Very shortly, you will see a shortage of foreign exchange in circulation.

Now, if everything changes, but our minds/mindsets do not change, how will we deal with the changes in demand. The old order cannot deal with the new order. The mind must be renewed each day that we may be able to accurately discern market in order to prevent loss and further problems in the economy.

The solutions that nations have been carrying out include:

1. Redundancy Exercises

2. Increasing Taxes

3. Capitalizing on Immorality

4. Giving waivers to foreign investors

5. Divesting the land and assets of the nation

6. Borrowing from International Lenders

7. Making decisions that affect mainly the Small Businesses and the Poor

All these decisions are nothing new and it will only create greater hardship for new businesses, new jobs, new ideas; we must embrace New Wine! It is time for us to try unconventional methods. Here is food for thought. The mind of the individual must grow before economy can grow. There is no way locally or globally, we can build on two (2) foundations.

At this juncture, we do not need any more statistics, research and documentation. We need action and results!

We need to ask some pertinent questions:

1. *Who controls the economy?*

2. *Who decides success or failure?*

In the same way that hurdling poverty begins in the mind, likewise economic change must first start in the mind. So, before that changes, the mind must change; when the mind changes, the speech will change; and when that changes, the environment will change and then our pockets will have more than change!

Without a mind change, regardless of the program we put in place, it is going to fail and put us into further debt.

How Do We Change The Mind

Before the minds of the people change, the minds of the leaders in every sector and category must change! Changes come through the Word of God, Prayer, Disaster and Adversity! Furthermore, we must look to the One Who controls change. (Psalms 121).

1. Did the Economic Model ascribed to our nation fit the needs of the nation and the time?

2. Are the programs implemented in our schools fit for the needs of the nation's children and the direction that the nation is headed?

If the mind does not change, rest assured, the sight cannot change.

We must remember a vision is also a function of the heart, not just the eyes, and all nations need a blueprint for economic change, in other words, they need a vision. If the mind is not renewed, how will we truly identify the value that exists within our nation, and catch hold of the vision which is to bring the nation out of its current state and into a place of prosperity and success. What do other countries see existing in our nation that we are not seeing? The old way of learning will not solve the mystery. Neither will we be able to discern what the priorities.

If our minds are not changed, then:

1. What will happen in the next 5 years regarding job creation?

2. In this present economic climate, how will governments collect taxes and at what expense?

3. What will happen to University Students who can no longer afford the education; and even when they graduate, who will employ them?

4. What will happen in the political arena when politicians employ the same strategies, and methods in a changing world?

"The Old Model Is Broken, We Need To Create A New One" – Ban Ki-Moon, Secretary General of the UN

"Worldwide, more than 400 million new jobs will be needed over the next decade. That means that policy-makers must get serious, now, about generating decent employment," said Secretary-General Ban Ki-moon at the high-level thematic debate on The State of the World Economy and Finance and its Impact on Development, held on 17 May. "It is time to recognize that human capital and natural capital are every bit as important as financial capital," he added.'" (May 17, 2012)

We need Vision, lest we perish!

Chapter 14

CLIMATE CHANGE BRINGS WEALTH TRANSFER

There are many discussions in the media and developing countries taking place in an effort to fully understand the issue of Climate Change. It is imperative for people to know that God, at times, has to send great earthquakes and other disasters – spiritually or naturally – in order to bring deliverance to His people from (spiritual or physical) chains, bonds, captivity, yokes (of bondage) and in some cases, prisons.

In Acts 16: 26, God sent a great earthquake to set His servants free. In the book of Exodus, we see ten (10) plagues – which we would regard as Climate Change. So, Climate Change is linked to the leadership style of kings, rebellion against God, the treatment of His people, and the accommodation of advisors who are involved in the occult.

While we will have pride, arrogance, injustice and enslavement of God's people, we will always have such climatic activities. Oftentimes, it is only in disasters that people will become free.

In Acts 16: 26, we see the foundation of the prison house shaken, then we see the door open to set the people free. It was after the foundation of the prison house was shaken that the door opened and the chains were unfastened. This shows us that for freedom opportunity and transfer of wealth to happen, there has to be a change of climate.

The Red Sea had to open in order to drown Pharaoh and his army, thereby releasing God's people completely from the bondage. Thereafter, God commanded them to borrow the gold.

God's people were being pursued by Pharaoh and his army, even after God made a way of escape for His people.

Haggai 2: 6 – 8 says, "For thus says the Lord of hosts: 'Once more (it is a little while) I will shake heaven and earth, the sea and dry land; and I will shake all nations, and they shall come to the Desire of All Nations, and I will fill this [b]temple with glory,' says the Lord of hosts. 'The silver is Mine, and the gold is Mine,' says the Lord of hosts.

This scripture speaks about Climate Change through wealth transfer from the rich to the poor. He outlines in this scripture that the gold and the silver belong to Him – the resources belong to Him; and because of unfair distribution and lack of sufficient resources available to establish His Kingdom, He would shake

1. Heaven (The 2nd Heaven)
2. The Earth
3. Sea, and
4. Dry Land.

He would also shake all nations – including the earthly Administrations. The desired wealth of all nations will come. An influx of people (treasure) as prophesied in Isaiah 60, filling His temple with His glory, has to do with building the Kingdom.

For too long, the world has been using God's gold and silver to fund anti-Christ systems, while failing to empower the people. The True Church will receive a transfer of God's resources to build His people. (1 Corinthians 6: 9 – 20), so that the focus will mainly be on the people, rather than solely on the infrastructure. I guarantee that many millionaires and billionaires will go broke unless they get into alignment and understand that the resource(s) in the earth belong to God - to good and not evil. There is going to be accountability for their stewardship.

Shaking

Earthquakes - physical and spiritual - are very symbolic. The quake is what God uses to overthrow the systems and foundations that result in the captivity and bondage of the people. The shaking will open doors and loose chains. The power of Prayer and Praise will bring a great earthquake and many will be free. Some may call it Climate Change, but the great city called Babylon (which was initially the Roman Empire) and its capital, symbolize the rise and fall of nations and empires throughout history. As you continue to pray and praise, watch out for a great earthquake - physically and spiritually - many captives will be set free!! (Revelation 16: 18; Acts 16: 26)

The Lord says that many buildings will be shaken, as many, instead of utilizing the wealth to help the poor, they created images and idols for them to worship. They created moles and bats.

Isaiah 2: 19 – 22 says, "They shall go into the holes of the rocks, and into the caves of the earth, from the terror of the Lord and the glory of His majesty, when He arises to shake the earth mightily. In that day a man will cast away his idols of silver and his idols of gold, which they made, each for himself to worship, to the moles and bats, to go into the clefts of the rocks, and into the crags of the rugged rocks, from the terror of the Lord and the glory of His majesty, when He arises to shake the earth mightily. Sever yourselves from such a man, whose breath is in his nostrils; for of what account is he?"

Many think they can protect themselves by erecting certain kinds and styles of buildings underground or in the air.

When the earth begins to shake or quake, it means that things are changing in the natural. Longstanding foundations are breaking down. Systems and laws are coming down. Things that are planted in the earth, God will use quakes, floods, and fires to bring change.

This is a warning also for leaders with the spirit of Pharaoh to be mindful that they too will be shaken down. (Ezekiel 31: 1 – 18)

God will use the shaking to promote new political leaders who are humble, while He removes those exalting themselves. (Ezekiel 21: 27)

Regardless of the weapons of mass destruction and other nuclear weapons that exist, we should never fear. God can use Climate Change to bring them down. So, while weapons of mass destruction affect Climate Change, we should never fear, because the earth will never be destroyed by such weaponry.

The book of Isaiah also speaks to us of the Mountain Principle. God shall establish, on top of the mountain, His earthly, Divine rule; one which stands forever, according to Daniel 2: 44.

2 Chronicles 7: 13 – 14 is very clear on Climate Change. God clearly tells us of the cause and the solutions for Climate Change. Prayer, Seeking God, Repentance and Humility will bring change and healing.

We also see in the Scriptures, that when the poor cry out, shaking takes place (Psalm 18: 6 – 7).

The Creation is looking to each of us, because it is our responsibility to bring Change to the Climate, (Romans 8: 19 – 21). The whole Creation, the Universe, have suffered the consequences of human sin being subjected to decomposition, futility and corruption; but the process is only temporary, because hope and deliverance is in Jesus Christ. So, Creation will be set free when man begins to walk in holiness and purity.

Revelation 16: 21 shows us that because of Man's behavior, apocalyptic events where the Seven (7) Seals open, we will see the size of the hail that will fall will weigh anywhere from 75 to 110 pounds.

Nahum 1: 1 – 15 tells us that God is in the wind and the whirlwind, and it shows us the judgement that will take place, as well as the spirit of Nimrod that will be in operation. (Genesis 10). It shows the power of God over Creation. He rebukes seas, dries up rivers and He is a stronghold in the times of trouble. There is no system that can stop God. He overthrows them and will create disasters to bless His people. (Matthew 24: 7, Luke 21: 11 and Luke 21: 25). Even the Land of Promise – Israel, will be shaken (Ezekiel 38: 19 and Joel 3: 16).

Chapter 15

FOLLOW INSTRUCTIONS - CHANGE YOUR ENVIRONMENT

Regardless of how foolish an instruction may seem, the key to overcoming certain obstacles in your life is to simply follow the instructions – whether spiritual or professional. **God will never give you an instruction which goes against His Word.**

Many times, I see people going through problems and God gives them simple instructions. Some may start the process and then become inconsistent and ultimately discontinue, while others may just ignore the instructions altogether. There are others who start the execution of the instructions but as soon as they see a little light in their circumstances, they abandon the instructions to run after the light and then because they did not follow through on the instructions, the problem returns and they are back at square one.

When problems come up, the Lord does not always use the same method to bring the solution to your situation. Not every problem requires long prayers and prophecies to get you past the problem. Some solutions come in the form of instructions from God that must be followed to get the complete breakthrough/victory. This is why the Lord has given the gifts of Word of Knowledge and Word of Wisdom – for direction. Again, God is not going to give you instructions that are opposite to or go against His Word.

When you go to the doctor you must follow the instructions given on the prescription in order to get the full benefit of healing. In legal matters, you must follow the instructions of the lawyer in order to be victorious in your case. In the same way, when you go to the servant of God for spiritual counseling and advice, you must also follow the instructions given. In all cases – Doctor, Lawyer, God's Servant – there is time that was spent to get the necessary instruction for you to follow for your benefit: It cost the doctor years of study and continuing education; it cost the lawyer their years of study and time to stay up-to-date with current laws in order to advise you well; and it cost the Servant of God time spent in the Presence of God, and in the Scriptures and maintaining a holy lifestyle to receive and maintain the anointing to hear from God and give you the right instructions for your situation. Your obedience to God's instructions bring peace, prosperity and the fulfillment of your purpose and also creates miracles. Otherwise you will never move forward past your last act of obedience. (Deuteronomy 28: 1 – 14; Proverbs 14: 12; John 14: 21; Joshua 7: 10 – 13; 1 Kings 17: 15 – 16; Hebrews 11: 11; Ephesians 6: 5 – 8 and 2 Kings 5)

When things are not going right in your life, check and see which instructions you did not follow. What if the leprous commander Naaman did not obey the instruction to dip 7 times in the Jordan? What if he had allowed his pride to cause him to disobey the instructions? You will never be a good leader until you learn to follow instructions; and here is the big key – YOU DO NOT HAVE TO UNDERSTAND HIS INSTRUCTIONS. For example, a person may be acting in a movie and the director gives an instruction on how to play a part. The director sees the vision for the movie much clearer than the actor does, so the actor only needs to follow the director's instructions. Likewise, when your boss gives you an instruction on the job, your role is to follow the instructions as long as those instructions do not go against the company's policies and guidelines. You are not the boss and you are not privy to what the boss knows concerning the organization's vision.

Remember, you can be given an instruction – both spiritually and naturally – just to see if you are willing to follow instructions.

Recurring problems happen because instructions are not followed. Political and governmental failure and defeat comes about when they refuse to follow instructions. Ministerial failure comes about when people refuse to obey the instructions given by God and the leader above them. Life becomes easier when we follow God's instructions and waste is reduced and eliminated. The world would be a much better place if we only learned to follow instructions. Discipline starts with following instructions. Our victory begins when we obey and carry out the instructions given.

Today, many struggle with immigration and having proper travel documents. It is a sore point for many. The enemy knows that there are certain places to which you must travel for business, work and/or family to be a blessing to others and to be blessed. The enemy will assign strongmen to hinder us from travelling to a particular place in a particular time. He will want to bring delay to the signing and approval of documents. He will want to hinder the signing, approval and/or processing of passports, petitions, visas, residencies and/or citizenships for example, to cause anxiety, stress, delay, loss of time and money.

In such cases, it is extremely to important to follow the instructions of the Lord, so that He can open doors of access for us, and allow us quick approval of Travel Documents.

Chapter 16

CHANGING THE ENVIRONMENT OF DIPLOMATIC IMMUNITY

Diplomats who represent their country abroad enjoy diplomatic immunity. This protects them against prosecution in the receiving state for the entire period in which they hold their diplomatic post. Article 31 of the Vienna Convention gives Diplomats every right to be protected including receiving exemption from taxes and court action.

Similarly, according to 2 Corinthians 5: 20 we have Spiritual Diplomatic Immunity. We are both citizens of heaven, and diplomats representing the Kingdom of God, meaning as Ambassadors, Satan cannot harass/persecute, or prosecute nor arrest us neither does he have the right to attack us with any witchcraft, demonic influence, legal issues, sickness, poverty because we have been forgiven of all our past and it has been protected.

Psalm 91 also gives us Diplomatic Immunity because we are called to do His work and we have a Divine Assignment to accomplish. Mark 16: 15 – 18 also gives us Global Diplomatic Immunity through the

Commission with full benefits. Matthew 28: 18 - 20 also gives us that Diplomatic Immunity.

As Diplomats, we have the right to be protected daily from sickness, untimely death, shame and disgrace. We have the right to be given favor, grace, Diplomatic Passports, Diplomatic Access. We have the right to be protected from earthly legal systems, based on the Scripture and the Vienna Convention 1978 – including safe passage daily.

According to Exodus 11: 1 – 7, we have the right to be protected from disaster and everything negative that happens in the world including riots, diseases, plagues, death or anything else, because the Lord has separated His people from others.

As Diplomats, we have the right to receive favor, mercy, compassion, grace and be covered under the Blood of Jesus. We also have the right to Angelic Escorts, the blessings of Deuteronomy 28: 1 – 14, when we obey the Lord God.

God gave His people Diplomatic Immunity according Genesis 35: 1 – 5 which says: "Then God said to Jacob, "Arise, go up to Bethel and dwell there; and make an altar there to God, who appeared to you when you fled from the face of Esau your brother." And Jacob said to his household and to all who were with him, "Put away the foreign gods that are among you, purify yourselves, and change your garments. Then let us arise and go up to Bethel; and I will make an altar there to God, who answered me in the day of my distress and has been with me in the way which I have gone." So, they gave Jacob all the foreign [a]gods which were in their hands, and the earrings which were in their ears; and Jacob hid them under the terebinth tree which was by Shechem. And they journeyed, and the terror of God was upon the cities that were all around them, and they did not pursue the sons of Jacob."

Chapter 17

FASTING AND THE ENVIRONMENT

There are a number of things we need to understand about the Environment. The Environment goes beyond the physical surroundings. In fact, your environment includes the physical and spiritual surroundings, and is a significant part of our existence that can influence every area of our lives and can be influenced by many aspects of our lives.

Creating and Changing Your Environment

You can create or change your environment by:

1. The words you speak

2. Your giving

3. Your Praise and Worship

4. Your act of obedience to God and His instructions (Deuteronomy 28:1 – 14)

5. Your Fasting and Prayer

6. With the sacrifices you make. What are you willing to do to see change within your family, church, community and your nation?

7. The daily choices you make. Sometimes we are looking for a crowd, but all we need is four good people.

8. The level of your faith in God. Your faith will cause obstacles to move, bring a revival, and break poverty.

Furthermore,

1. You will never see change until you become frustrated and fed up with your present environment.

2. If are comfortable with where you are spiritually, you will never change your environment. But if you truly want change, are you willing to pray three (3) times per day including Fourth (4th) watch between the hours of 3 a.m. - 6 a.m.

3. If you are desperate for change as a single person in getting married, are you willing to fast until your clothes fall off? Are you willing to give up food that everyone craves?

4. The only difference between current and the past great men that were in the Bible is they were willing to wrestle with God to bless them, to change their environment and their circumstances. They would wrestle all night with God. Many of us will talk but we do not walk the walk. We often complain more than we fast, we will agree with the enemy more than we fight, we talk more than we pray.

5. Every time God is going to bless, He gives an instruction. What are you willing to do differently to see that change?

6. Every time we see change in the Bible, there is always something done differently. For example:

   i.   The woman with the issue of blood pushed past the crowd: she did not allow her uncleanness or her lack of resources and brokenness to hinder her from getting to Jesus, she pushed past the crowd and got her healing.

   ii. Zacchaeus did not allow his height or stature to hinder him, he climbed the tree to get to Jesus. He didn't watch the crowd - he pushed past the crowd.

iii.   The blind man cried - he pushed past the crowd to get Jesus' attention.

iv.   Four men in Luke 5: 17 - 33 climbed through the roof to get Jesus' attention and it brought healing.

There is always something in our midst to use to change our environment. What are you not seeing or what are you not doing?   In order to change your environment and to receive God's power you must do something different.   Never watch the crowd - push past the crowd! Never allow the crowd to keep you in your present environment. (Mark 2: 1 – 12)

Both the Old and New Testaments teach us the value of Fasting. Fasting about denying one's self including abstaining from food, drink and so on, to focus on the things of God.

God used Fasting to break yokes (Isaiah 58), break curses, break bondage, set captives free, loose the oppressed, break cycles, give justice, reveal supernatural revelation, getting answers.   Fasting helps us to grow and strengthen us as a Christian. There are certain things we cannot achieve in life without fasting. The Bible said we should not Fast for strife, to compete or for wrong motives.   Through Prayer and Fasting we can break strongholds.

Fasting overthrows the enemy's plan and gives us protection. Ensure that you seek permission, if you are married, when you are about to Fast. Seek consent from your spouse to avoid any temptation (1 Corinthians 7: 5). One of the best pieces of advice I can give you is to get your spouse involved when you are Fasting. Unity in Fasting brings miracles. Try to avoid any denial of sexual intercourse if your spouse is unsaved. It is not recommended that married couples to do long fasting such as 40 day fasting, as this can bring temptation. Also seek your physician's advice if you have a health condition before you start a fast.

What Fasting Is Really About

Fasting is denying yourself of a basic necessity, or something you enjoy such as food. You can fast and cease having soda, coffee, pastry, chocolate, candy and other sweets for the period you are Fasting; you can eat vegetables and drink water instead. You would do this in order to receive something of even greater value to you. So, you would for example, put aside certain foods as you seek the Lord for greater blessing.

Generally, you can begin your fast at midnight and break it at either midday, 1 p.m. or 3 p.m. Some fasts go from 6 a.m. – 6 p.m. on the same day. There are various Fasts, outlined below, ranging from one (1) day to Forty (40) days. In the Book of Acts 14: 23, the Church **fasted** for Ordination, for God's blessing and approval. God is calling the local church back to Fasting before the Act of Ordination. This is significant in the process of selecting leaders.

Repentance Fast

1 Samuel 7: 6 tells us of a **Repentance Fast**. During this Fast, the people put away strange gods and the idols Baalim and Ashtaroth. There cannot be repentance without first putting away the idols in our lives.

The people fasted on that day and as they realized that the condition that they were in was due to the fact that they turned from the True and Living God, and because of the Fast, they received victory over the Philistines. We cannot fast while we are still holding on to our idols.
The Repentance Fast was the fast King David did in 2 Samuel 1:12, when great men were falling.

Fast for Ministerial Direction and Appointment

In Acts 13: 2, there is a Fast for Ministerial Direction and Appointment of Leaders. (1 King 19: 8). The prophet Elijah fasted 40 days in the wilderness, after being pursued by Jezebel. Also, both Jesus and Moses fasted for 40 days - a total fast without food or water (Luke 4: 2 - 4, Exodus 34: 28).

Sanctification and Consecration Fast

We also see a Fasting take place in Exodus 19: 15 – 17 where they fasted and abstained from sexual activity in order to receive a visitation from God. This is a Sanctification and Consecration Fast. These three days of abstaining were in order to prepare for God's Visitation and Presence; the people were instructed to purify themselves both physically and spiritually. They were told to separate themselves from their spouses in order to receive from God.

Sexual relations normally involve your whole being, and will distract you from the Sanctification process as you seek God. It is encouraged that married couples, in accordance with 1 Corinthians 7: 5, to abstain from sex for a short period of time, in order to devote themselves to God in Prayer and Fasting. So, each time one is threatened by the enemy, we must Fast because it impacts the spiritual realm and releases angels bringing answers and solutions, as well as bringing down strongmen and strongholds, just as in the 21-day Daniel Fast. Fasting changes your circumstances, and it is more about focus than it is about food. It brings you closer to God and that is why your motives must be right when you Fast. David prayed and fasted over his sick child in 2 Samuel 12: 16.

We must fast to get God's favor and His deliverance from demonic oppression according Mark 9: 21 – 29. Matthew 13: 58 outlines that not all demonic bondage responds to deliverance (or what some call exorcism), but some deliverances only comes through fervent prayer and fasting, so fasting provides a climate of faith that brings deliverance.

Prayer and Fasting

1. Gives Us Power,
2. Increases Our Faith,
3. Brings Healing,
4. Strengthens Our Belief In Jesus,
5. Gives Us Grace, and
6. Creates Miracles.

Other Fasts

In Daniel 10: 3, we see him embarking on a 21-day Fast. During that Fast, the Scripture says, Daniel ate no choice food, no meat, no wine, no lettuce, no bread. We could also say no make-up especially for the women, this would classify as a partial fast.

Esther 4: 15 – 16 shows us that the Esther Fast is a 3-day total fast, which means that during the three days, nothing is consumed – no food nor water.

Joel 2 speaks of the Repentance Fast. Nehemiah 1: 4 – 11 Nehemiah fasted for his country, the spiritual condition, for divine intervention, for repentance. We see the same in Daniel 9: 4 and Ezra 9: 6, that the same is required for national repentance, restoration, favor and mercy.

When We Fast

1. In Luke 2:37 we see where Anna was consecrated, she lived in the temple and served God with prayer and fasting. Anna was a prophetess.

2. Psalm 69:10. When one is going through suffering for endurance, you fast.

3. In Psalm 35: 13 – 14. David fasted to receive healing for others.

4. In Daniel 9: 3 – 5, there is a fast that every political leader should do for the condition of their country. Every congress/parliament should do this fast. They have to bear the sin of the nation and confess the sin for change to take

place within a nation. Daniel never excluded himself from the condition that was taking place, but he included himself, hence even the people who vote for leaders who turn away from God have to repent and fast, because all sin is directed towards God. So every prophet, king, princes, the people, have to fast for God's mercy.

5. 2 Samuel 12:16 – 17 David fasted and cried out to God after committing adultery and bringing conception of a child. Today, the same thing happens within families and many refuse to fast for healing and restoration.

6. 1 Kings 21: 25 – 27 we see the king fast and cried out when Elijah pronounced judgement on him. King Ahab allowed his wife to stir him up to perform wickedness. So, because Ahab cried out, God did not bring evil on him - the judgement was differed.

7. The Apostle Paul did a 3-day fast when he was struck down by God. He consumed no food nor water. This was a complete (total) fast like an Esther Fast. This Fast, brought restoration to his physical and spiritual sight (Acts 9: 9 and Esther 4: 15 – 16).

Furthermore, you can also Fast from Social Network and Television.

Fasting is one of the keys to releasing your deliverance, not just at the individual level, but also at the national level – where we proclaim a Fast in which the entire nation participates. We must fast when there is an urgent situation and also against attacks. (2 Chronicles 4: 11). We must also fast when our country is threatened by invasion as is seen in 2 Chronicles 20: 3; and this is a good fast for nations threatened by war. Furthermore, when Spiritual Warfare is coming against us as the Church, we must remember what happened after the 2 Chronicles 20: 3 Fast, where God gave instructions and as the people obeyed the enemies were defeated. (2 Chronicles 20: 24 – 27). This Fast is effective especially when more than one enemy has joined forces to come against your family, your church, and your nation.

In 2 Chronicles 20: 3, the king depended on God to intervene and defeat his enemies. What if today's political leaders and church leaders would fast? We would have great reward and great benefit!

So,

1. A 3-day Fast will break curses, infirmities and poverty. Fasting brings creative miracles in our bodies and also in the nation. (2 Kings 6 & 7). We

must recognize that there is no shortage of money in the world, we only have a distribution problem because it is in the hands of the wrong people. Fasting changes the climate that changes the hearts of men to re-adjust the distribution of wealth.

2. There is a night fast where the king fasted for Daniel. This can be done from 6 p.m. to 6 a.m. the next morning.

3. The Isaiah 58: 5 Fast is a powerful and effective Fast for every Christian's life. Jesus taught that some things are only resolved by prayer and fasting. Fasting and Spiritual Holiness are acceptable to God when we have our priorities straight – for example, sharing with the hungry, sheltering the homeless and clothing the naked and caring for our whole family despite our personal or individual circumstances. This is the prerequisite of Godliness. Fasting becomes offensive in God's sight when we ignore the people closest to his heart – the Poor, the Oppressed and the Needy (Proverbs 21: 8 – 9, Luke 4: 17 – 19). God wants us to fast in order to loose the bonds of wickedness from the nation and from the people. We need to Fast regarding Social Injustice, Economic Problems, the Breaking of Strongholds from international

lenders and the Oppression of poorer countries, Debt Cancelation.

Chapter 18

THE POWER OF PRAYER

Matthew 6: 9-13 tell us that prayer reduces debt, gives daily provision, bring God's will to pass, and causes what takes place in the heavens to also take place on the earth. Prayer gives us natural and spiritual sustenance, power and protects us from evil.

According to Luke 21-22 and I Kings 18: 36-46, prayer opens the heavens (and the world needs an open heaven right now). An open heaven means that healing, solutions, changes and strengthening will take place.

Prayer changes God's heart (2 Kings 20:1-7) and brings healing. Prayer caused God to add 15 years to a king's life after he had decided to take his life away.

Prayer delivers a nation in times of war and gives it victory and allows the nation to collect the spoils. (2 Chronicles 20:1-13).

It is noteworthy that in I Timothy 2:8, God outlines that man should pray everywhere – nowhere is exempt. When this happens, then we will see a global change in businesses, various organizations and in individuals' lives and homes.

Prayer allows us to be bold; it breaks plots and gives you victory over your enemies. (Ephesians 6:18-20; Proverbs 6:7-10; Psalms 109:4)

For all the nations that will be going to the polls, public relations and campaign strategies, monetary strength, slander, undermining and idolatry will not bring victory. It will be prayer.

Those that are going through hardship will be wiser in their prayer. The more difficult times become, the more people will pray. The more people pray, the stronger they become, and the better able they are to handle their problems.

Jehovah Tsebaoth

The Lord functions in innumerable capacities and the names of God are descriptive of His character and tells of the role He is playing when we call Him by each name. We need to know which name to call when we need His help.

'Jehovah Tsebaoth' means 'The Lord of Hosts'. This is the Lord that wages war and renders service unto God. He deals with Spiritual Warfare. It was in this capacity the function when He made the sun go backwards ten (10) degrees – when Joshua commanded the sun to stand still. (Joshua 10: 12 – 13)

God has power over the sun, the moon and all the elements of Heaven – He created it all; and there are times when we are fighting wars, the environment must obey us, not work against us! We cannot eliminate the supernatural. The Lord of Hosts is over all realms – natural and supernatural!

In Judges 4, the children of Israel were facing grievous threats. King Jabin, wanted to destroy God's people. There was also a mighty General whose name was Sisera, who had many iron chariots. In fact, he had over 900 chariots of iron and for many years he harshly oppressed the children of Israel. For Deborah and Barak to go up against such a force was an impossible task. But they called upon **Jehovah Tsebaoth**. The Lord routed all of his chariots and his entire army with the edge of the sword. The Lord confused Sisera and his army by curtailing the mobility of his chariots through the flooding of the Kishon River. God caused a massive storm and defeated Sisera's superior armed forces.

There are some King Jabins and some great Sisera-like oppositions that come against us from time to time. In Judges 5 you will see the testimony of the Great God! Regardless of how powerful and how rich your enemies are, or how difficult the situation is, we have the authority to call legions of angels (which is at least 72,000) to bring deliverance.

The following Scriptures show our authority over the angels:

Psalm 68: 17

Psalm 103: 21

Hebrews 1: 14

II Kings 18: 5

Prayer Reminders

The Word of the Lord reminds us what prayer can do and why we need to pray. His Word says as follows:

Matthew 14: 23, "After he had dismissed them, he went up on a mountainside by himself to pray. Later that night, he was there alone"

Luke 5: 16, "But Jesus often withdrew to lonely places and prayed."

Psalms 2: 8, "Ask me, and I will make the nations your inheritance, the ends of the earth your possession."

Matthew 9: 37 – 38, "Then he said to his disciples, "The harvest is plentiful but the workers are few. Ask the

Lord of the harvest, therefore, to send out workers into his harvest field."

Mark 11: 25, "And when you stand praying, if you hold anything against anyone, forgive them, so that your Father in heaven may forgive you your sins."

Proverbs 21:13, "Whoever shuts their ears to the cry of the poor will also cry out and not be answered.

Secrets behind Successful Praying

Prayer does not have to be boring or frustrating. Prayer with music can help you create an environment conducive to His Presence, our Worship, and afford us victory. Furthermore, prophetic actions and declarations can help to encourage your prayer life and keep you in His Presence. Know that:

1. The Lord is calling us to pray at least 3 times per day. It is not a sin to pray.

2. Prayer puts fear in the heart of Satan

3. Prayer is your greatest weapon

4. Prayer changes you first, and brings peace and strength to you on a daily basis

5. Prayer is the key to power

6. Prayer breaks prison gates and set the captives free

7. Prayer pleases the heart of God and gives you authority

8. Prayer blesses others

9. Prayer opens the door for God to show us great and mighty things

10. Prayer gives you access

Matthew 11: 28 says, "Come to me, all you who are weary and burdened, and I will give you rest."

1 Timothy 2:1 – 4 also state, "I urge, then, first of all, that petitions, prayers, intercession and thanksgiving be made for all people — for kings and all those in authority, that we may live peaceful and quiet lives in all godliness and holiness. This is good, and pleases God our Savior, who wants all people to be saved and to come to a knowledge of the truth.

When you lift others and their needs before God, God will release your needs. We will see change.

Job 42: 10 shows us that after Job had prayed for his friends, the Lord restored his fortunes and gave him twice as much as he had before. Pray for your friends and God will multiply your blessings.

Jeremiah 33: 3 says, "Call to me and I will answer you and tell you great and unsearchable things you do not know."

Guide to Daily Prayer

1. Pray in public worship and pray in services with other believers.

2. Pray in private (Matthew 14:23; Luke 5:16)

3. Pray for the Head of your nation and all national leaders and Heads of States.

4. Pray for your leader every day, Apostle, his/her family, and every leader

5. Pray for the USA, the Caribbean, and other countries that God tells you.

6. Pray for souls, for unbelievers to be saved (the lost/unsaved); if we do not pray for them, they will die and go to HELL. (Psalms 2: 8)

7. Pray for laborers to gather the souls into the church and work in ministry (Matthew 9:37 – 38)

8. Pray for World Evangelism and Revival to take place

9. Pray for all new converts; ask the Lord to keep them in His way and will. Pray that they will always have the zeal and desire to read the Word of God; and that they will keep coming into His house.

10. Pray for the Lord to remove unforgiveness from the heart so that your prayers will not be hindered, and so your prayers will be answered (Mark 11:25).

11. Pray against a lack of generosity, especially within the Body of Christ. (Proverbs 21:13)

12. Pray for your boss/supervisor/employer at your workplace and pray for your workplace for lost souls to be saved. That's your key to promotion.

Chapter 19

THE PURPOSE OF FORGIVENESS AND PRAYER

What can stop God from not answering your prayer?

Forgiveness is powerful, yet it is difficult for most of us, especially most Christians. That is likely due to a misconception of the true meaning and purpose of Forgiveness. God wants us to forgive. Forgiveness can open the door to your promotion.

Mercy is part of forgiveness as well and it is hardly practiced. There is no mercy or compassion in the heart of persons these days and times. Forgiveness is pardon, remission of sins, mercy, clemency, reprieve, and even amnesty.

Forgiveness is not easy especially when it is sabotage, being lied upon, or even deep seeded hurt. It can hinder you from moving forward with God. We all need the Father to forgive us, because it was you and I that crucified Him. It was our sins that nailed Him to the cross.

Matthew 6: 14 – 15 says, "For if you forgive men their trespasses, your heavenly Father will also forgive you.

<u>But if you do not forgive men their trespasses, neither will your Father forgive your trespasses."</u>

If we do not forgive then God will not forgive us. Forgiveness is free, it is what is required of us. Many persons, including Christians, walk with un-forgiveness and refuse to let go; this, in itself, hinders us from moving forward with trust. Forgiveness is not only for those who were wronged but for all involved. You must give up your right which is not a sign of weakness. You must let God defend you! Sometimes trying to defend yourself will complicate things. The process of forgiveness includes forgiveness, reconciliation, and even restoration/deliverance. Every level that we go we must extend a deeper level of forgiveness to others; or even for your own mistakes and burdens that you are carrying. We must forgive ourselves, family members. We must stop comparing what should be, what should not be, what should have been and even what would have been.

Every time you compare your life it hurts you, as it contrasts a current state versus a former state and holds you back. You cannot go forward looking backwards. Release is necessary when it comes to forgiveness. Lot's wife could not release the wealth and kept looking back and turned into a pillar of salt. It is a process and forgiveness is surgery of the soul, not a condition. Forgiving someone does not mean that the person has changed; but instead you have released them spiritually for the wrong that was caused.

Forgiveness & Prayer

Matthew 18: 21 – 35 says, "Then Peter came to Jesus and asked, "Lord, how many times shall I forgive my brother or sister who sins against me? Up to seven times?" Jesus answered, "I tell you, not seven times, but seventy-seven times. "Therefore, the kingdom of heaven is like a king who wanted to settle accounts with his servants. As he began the settlement, a man who owed him ten thousand bags of gold was brought to him. Since he began the settlement, a man who owed him ten thousand bags of gold was brought to him. Since he was not able to pay, the master ordered that he and his wife and his children and all that he had be sold to repay the debt. "At this the servant fell on his knees before him. 'Be patient with me,' he begged, 'and I will pay back everything.' The servant's master took pity on him, canceled the debt and let him go. "But when that servant went out, he found one of his fellow servants who owed him a hundred silver coins. He grabbed him and began to choke him. 'Pay back what you owe me!' he demanded. "His fellow servant fell to his knees and begged him, 'Be patient with me, and I will pay it back.' "But he refused. Instead, he went off and had the man thrown into prison until he could pay the debt. When the other servants saw what had happened, they were outraged and went and told their master everything that had happened. "Then the master called the servant in. 'You wicked servant,' he said, 'I canceled all that debt of yours because you begged me to. Shouldn't you have had mercy on your fellow servant just as I had on you?' In anger his master handed him over to the jailers to be tortured, until he should pay back all he owed. "This is how my heavenly Father will treat each of you unless you forgive your brother or sister from your heart."

When God bestows favor, He will require the same mercy, compassion, and forgiveness to be extended from you as was extended to you. When we do not extend forgiveness as we have received, the Lord, Himself, will "throw you in prison" – allow us to fall into bondage again.

God always turn around the bad things into good things. When God is going to promote us, He sends someone into our life. When the devil wants to destroy us, he brings someone to distract us. The enemy at times assigns someone in our life to bring us down. It is always a spiritual thing.

How Do You Forgive Yourself?

The first key to Forgiveness is Repentance, both inward and outward. Forgiveness comes with condition. Jesus recognized that there had to be conditions that needed to be fulfilled before Forgiveness can be granted. Forgiveness is part of a mutual relationship, and Repentance with the offender. God does not forgive without repentance. The effect of Forgiveness is to restore, to its former state, the relationship that was broken because of sin. Such restoration requires the cooperation of both parties. There must be both a granting and an acceptance of Forgiveness. When we make mistakes, sometimes it is a challenge to get past the point of why we made the choice to begin with. Again, we must release, get past, and forgive ourselves. We must forgive us.

2 Corinthians 5:16 – 17 says, "Therefore, from now on, we regard no one according to the flesh. Even though we have known Christ according to the flesh, yet now we know Him thus no longer. Therefore, if anyone is in Christ, he is a new creation; old things have passed away; behold, all things have become new."

All things have become new, the only thing that God cannot remember is our sin. It is in the Sea of

Forgetfulness. You are already forgiven – it is by faith. Do not let the enemy harass you. Do not let the enemy revive a part of you that is no longer active. Know your legal right – spiritually and naturally. You are a new being in Christ; do not let the enemy rob you. The Lord has already forgiven you of your past sins and you have received His forgiveness by faith. Do not bring it up again.

Do not wait on a feeling or a sound to know if you are forgiven or not. The enemy likes to condition you to think that there has to be a physical observation that you are forgiven; or "feel it in your system" - that is not so. The only thing you need to do is to know and believe that God is a true and faithful God; He is true to His word and has proven Himself to you in so many ways each and every day. The enemy uses... **"Do you feel forgiven? Have you heard a prophetic word?"** Know that you are forgiven, you must move on, God is on to bigger and greater things with you.

Ephesians 4:31-32 tells us, "Get rid of all bitterness, rage and anger, brawling and slander, along with every form of malice. Be kind and compassionate to one another, forgiving each other, just as in Christ God forgave you." All these things come through the door of Unforgiveness. 90% off the world believe that you can never ever change. The whole world is created not to forgive. Unforgiveness is what really holds up the blessing - your prayers will not be answered if there is Unforgiveness.

Unforgiveness,

1. Hinders our prayers being answered. True deliverance cannot come to you if you do not forgive yourself.

2. Restricts what God wants to do in your life, and takes circumstances to an undesirable level.

3. Exacts toil on your body, mind, and every emotion.

4. Hinders the power of bind and loose in your life.

5. Hinders you from walking in the power the God wants you to walk in.

The person who hurt you does not determine your blessing, God does. God is the One Who releases your blessing. Bless those who curse you. If you want God to deal with your enemies, just ask God to bless you. The Prayer of the Blessing cancel the curse they would want to release upon you.

Matthew 18: 21 – 22 tells us, "Then Peter came to Him and said, "Lord, how often shall my brother sin against me, and I forgive him? Up to seven times?" Jesus said to him, "I do not say to you, up to seven times, but up to seventy times seven."

70×7=490 times per day per person of Forgiveness. Forgiving a person does not have to do with your having physical access to them. God is telling us to forgive and pardon others because you have been forgiven.

The Significance of 70

The number 70 is the number which signifies perfection, completeness, period of judgement, perfect spiritual order. We have seen the number 70 mentioned several times in the Bible – 61 times to be exact.

- ✓ In Numbers 11: 16, God told Moses to gather 70 Elders

- ✓ 70 is the number of people that had spiritual meal with God in Exodus 24: 9 - 11

- ✓ 70 elders were appointed by Moses.

- ✓ 70 is also the number of captivity where ancient Israel spent a total of 70 years according to Jeremiah 29: 10 – 12.

✓ In Daniel 9: 24 we see that there were 70 weeks to make an end of sin and finish transgressions, to make reconciliation for iniquity.

✓ In Luke 10, 70 disciples were sent out by Jesus to preach the gospel.

✓ Israel started a nation, when Joseph rose to power with 70 persons.

✓ The Bible speaks of 70 parables that Jesus spoke.

✓ God showed Ezekiel 70 elders sinning.

✓ God said that man should live 70 years (Psalm 90: 10)

✓ Jacob had 70 descendants (Exodus 1:5).

✓ God dispersed 70 people in Genesis 10.

✓ People mourned for 70 days in Genesis 50:3.

✓ They refer to Jesus as 'man' 70 times in the New Testament.

Scripturally speaking, the number 70 represents Purity and Restoration; it is the number for breakthrough and fulfillment of authority, break curses and cycles in your life.   It is also the number 70 as appointment, anointing and the Spirit of Prophecy.

It is important to note that the word yoke is used 70 times in the Bible. In Galatians 5:1 and Galatians 2: 4 we see yoke and bondage, God will set the captives free from enslavement and confinement. Matthew 16: 19 says that God will give us the keys of the kingdom of heaven to bind and to loose.

We have the authority to break every bondage related to us. We can sow a seed of $70.00 and declare that every bondage and captivity is broken. The enemy has been using the different chains to confine God's people. There are many chains that exist, we have to ensure that regardless of what chains and bondage the enemy has us in, whether chains of lack, poverty, cycles, adultery, fornication, envy, jealousy, lack of opportunity, by sowing $70.00 God will turn captivity into opportunity and blessing.

Chapter 20

GRACE, FAVOR AND MERCY – UNUSUAL CLIMATE CHANGERS

We often talk about Grace, Favor and Mercy, but do we really understand what these words mean? No one can live without **Grace**. The obstacles, challenges and problems we face on a daily basis, could not/cannot be resolved without Grace, Favor and Mercy.

The word "Grace" simply put, means "getting something we do not deserve; unmerited favor; mercy and compassion."

God's Greatest Act

Grace that has been given/extended to us is the ability to receive salvation which is available through faith. (Ephesians 2: 8 – 9). Grace is what opens doors to us when we are not qualified and gives us promotion we do not even deserve. That is why we must be humble on a daily basis and show someone mercy and compassion; without Grace, we would not be in the position we are now.

Have you ever been in a selection process for a position or a competition of any kind? In your mind, you never thought you would reach very far or had the talent to go through it, or would even get to a certain level; but it was Grace that allowed you to come out on top and it even surprised you!

Oftentimes there are persons who are involved in accidents of one kind or another, and they are the only ones to survive. Some people will tell them they are lucky, but it is not luck – it is the Grace of Jesus Christ that kept them and has given them another chance. The main reason that you are alive now and are able read this very article is the Grace of God!

Favor occurs when the requirements and protocols are waived for you. For example, Esther, Daniel and Joseph all walked in great favor and the kings loved or became endeared to them. When we were going to school, some students, or maybe you, were called the 'Teacher's Pet'. God gave favor with the teacher. Maybe when everybody else was failing you just zoomed right through every class and exam with flying colors.

Mercy occurs when one deserves punishment and God withholds His hand and instead extends His love to them. For example, God sparing Jamaica from a category 5 hurricane; or in the legal circles, God would allow a magistrate to rule in your favor rather than against you; or in any organization with which you transact business; when you are in default, mercy is extended to you to settle the matter by way of a Grace period.

Gifts and Talents

Quite often, many will see the gifts and talents of others and shower them with praises and accolades! Look at people like Michael Jordan, Patrick Ewing, Usain Bolt, Bob Marley, Serena Williams and President Barack Obama. It is God's Grace and His Favor!

Know that NO LEADER at any level can truly be successful without God's Grace, Favor and Mercy; and that is what will bring prosperity within a nation. Every leader has to ensure that God's Grace, Favor and Mercy never leaves them, for when they do, there is sure defeat!

Success, growth and great achievement can only come through Grace. (John 15: 5) This is why we MUST abide in God. Regardless of how successful a person is, without God's grace, the qualifications and academic achievements mean nothing.

Many times, the success of an organization hinges on the presence of a few righteous people in the organization who have Grace and Favor on their lives! We see it with Jacob where Laban prospered simply by having Jacob working for him. Oftentimes, when the few righteous leave, the organization crashes or goes through a slow, painful death. So, extending Grace to a servant of God can save your life. They are your insurance; and that is why you must be careful in how you treat a servant of God.

Paul reminds us, in I Corinthians 15: 9–10, that although he is the least of the Apostles, it is the Grace of God that has allowed him to accomplish all the work the Lord allowed him to do for Him.

There are many times people will take on Titles and put themselves in certain positions; but it is the Grace of God that sanctions it all. So if God's grace for the title or position is not with you then do not take it on; you will be heading for trouble!

God wants to extend Grace, Favor and Mercy particularly to those who are sick – to heal their bodies. You need to begin praying for Grace, Favor and Mercy on a daily basis – for your family, community, nation and the nation's leaders.

Chapter 21

BREAKING EVIL ALTARS

An evil altar is a place where negotiations are carried out on behalf of someone to execute evil actions, set curses and yokes upon someone. Upon these altars they carry out sacrifices to their gods and pronounce evil decrees and curses against others.

Evil altars are physical and spiritual and are erected in several ways. Physically, they can be trees, rocks, images, rivers, forests, a family shrine or even a place in a house dedicated for that purpose. Evil altars can be set up in towns/cities, crossroads/intersections where the power of darkness manifests in that particular area. All those altars require satanic priests, agents who carry out sacrifices – including blood sacrifices – and utilize personal items of the person(s) they target. So, we must ask the Lord to destroy those altars. (Judges 16: 23, 2 Samuel 5: 19 – 21, Numbers 23: 1 – 2, 1 Kings 13)

Many of the sufferings we go through are the result of evil altars that have been established against us, because no evil can be executed without an altar and in the same way that the Lord would dispatch His angelic beings when we establish the altars of righteousness, the demonic forces are sent forth from the evil altars.

Let us pray aggressively against these altars.

The Most High/El Elyon Fast

This is a 10-day Family Fast where we declare Psalm 91 7 times daily for the duration of the Fast. We also study Daniel 1, especially verses 11 - 14

There are 4 Ps on which we focus during this Fast:

1. **Purpose** – where we Fast for God to direct us on what we need to do to fulfill our purpose for Him

2. **Prayer** – where we engage in improving and increase our prayer life.

3. **Perception** – our mindset – the way we think, particularly regarding the things of God, His Word and His instructions.

4. **Power** – where we ask the Lord to cause to walk in the power He has given us to accomplish His will and our purpose for Him.

Prayer Points/Requests:

That God will:

1. Lift us and our children above all those we lead financially, spiritually, physically – with power and favor.

2. Lift us and our children above all health issues, infirmities, affliction, sickness, disease, in all areas.

3. Lift us up above all cycles – witchcraft, divination, financial problems and generation curses.

4. Lift up our personal ministry and break the strongholds affecting the finance and growth of our church

5. Lift us and our children above all the enemies who want to destroy us, and grant us favor with kings, VIPs and with God Himself.

6. Lift us up and send Divine Destiny Helpers with pure hearts and motives toward us, our children and our church who will lift up our hands and will not be easily moved by the enemy.

7. Restore the family relationships with fathers and sons

8. Lift us and our children higher than all circumstances and mountains.

9. Give us more wisdom and knowledge, visions, skills in literature, interpretation and we will be 10 times better than magicians and astrologers. (Daniel 1: 17 – 20)

Each time the Fast is broken for the 10 days, eat only Vegetables and Fruits and drink only Water. Those with health issues must get the go-ahead from their medical professional, and fruit juices can be added to their meals during the Fast.

The Fast begins at midnight (no eating from midnight until the fast is to be broken.

Before breaking the Fast, you **must** pray.

Chapter 22

CALL THINGS INTO BEING

(As it is written, "I have made you a father of many nations") in the presence of Him whom he believed— God, who gives life to the dead and calls those things which do not exist as though they did" Romans 4:17.

As children of God, by utilizing our faith, we have the authority to call things into being. Everything we see in the natural is a result of someone calling it into being. Whatever you want without seeing it yet, you have the authority to call it into being if you believe

"For assuredly, I say to you, whoever says to this mountain, 'Be removed and be cast into the sea,' and does not doubt in his heart, but believes that those things he says will be done, he will have whatever he says." Mark 11:23

"And whatever things you ask in prayer, believing, you will receive" Matthew 21:22.

Calling things into being includes names, person, places and things. We must list what we want which we do not have and call them into being. When we are calling things we should not doubt, never doubt, because the word shall not return empty or void. The manifestation of what we call shall come to pass; the purpose of God shall take place. Success shall take place (Isaiah 55:11). We are not called to live by natural things alone but by the word that comes from the mouth of God. Our tongue is the key to our prosperity. Remember when we speak, it will manifest from the invisible to the visible, we have to call it. We may not see it with our spiritual eyes but we will soon see it once we call it with our physical eyes. If you can see it with your spiritual eyes, the picture God shows you, then you can call it into being.

<u>"We having the same spirit of faith, according as it is written, I believed, and therefore have I spoken; we also believe, and therefore speak"</u> (2 Corinthians 4:13)

In Genesis 1:1-31 we see where God speaks to the base things of the world – the despised, low things which are regarded as nothing. Furthermore, according to Genesis 1:1, He brought forth things that were non-existent by speaking them into existence. He spoke, "Let there be light" and there was light, thus God shows us that when we speak light we get light; and light signifies direction.

1. Romans 10:17 says faith comes by hearing the Word of God.

2. Ezekiel 12:25 says speak the word.

3. Hebrews 11:1 speaks of how faith is, we must begin to confess words of faith in our environment.

4. Romans 10:9 shows that our confession brings salvation, it also brings healing.

5. Psalm 33:9 said God spoke it and it came to be.

Matthew 17: 20 says <u>"So Jesus said to them, "Because of your [a]unbelief; for assuredly, I say to you, if you have faith as a mustard seed, you will say to this mountain, 'Move from here to there,' and it will move; and nothing will be impossible for you."</u>

If you do not like the direction your life is going, do something about it! Use your tongue to change your environment. The spiritual realm is only affected by words, sounds and language. Remember this, the rich are not generally negative in their thoughts and conversation, the rich are always positive.

Begin to list your goals and declare them and you shall have them, declare what you would want to have and you will see the manifestation. When you are declaring your blessing, declare the manifestation of resources for those who have the best interest of the poor, the "Third World" Nations, the nations of Africa, the islands of the Caribbean, Latin

American Nations at heart; and want to see all nations prosper.

Turning Negative Ds Into Positive Dominion

There are many negative things in life that begin with the letter D – many negative things that the enemy tends to use against us which causes pain, delay, loss of money, suffering, loneliness and robs us of our joy, peace and happiness.

The Lord wants us to be happy and have peace, but the enemy wants us - especially those who work for God – to be constantly unhappy.

I believe that most words that begin with the letter D have the most negative happenings. Some nations, like China, believe that the fourth letter of the alphabet is the unluckiest one. But as God's people, we can use the number four (4) which represents *"rule, reign, the four corners of the world, the four winds, dominion/dominions"*. We must ask God to cancel all the negative 'D's operating against us or in our lives!

Take a look at some of the negative 'D's that come against us.

Debt	Death	Denial
Delay	Disappointment	Destruction
Discouragement	Deception	Damning
Defeat	Diabetes	Diabolical
Dictator	Discord	Disobedience
Distress	Decrease	Doom
Devil	Doubt	Demons
Disgrace	Division	Depravity
Disillusionment	Disrespect	Degradation
Delinquency	Disorganization	Divorce

It is time for us to *Denounce* and *Deactivate* these Debilitating 'D's from our lives, and walk in **Dominion**.

Chapter 23

BIRTHING AND SPIRITUAL WARFARE

Our goal in Spiritual Warfare must always be to win and the key to winning in warfare is listening to and obeying God's instructions daily. That is why we must get into God's presence and avoid the daily distractions that the enemy tries to use against us. Each time there is a birthing about to take pace, it is always surrounded by heavy warfare.

Birthing

From the Spiritual perspective, Birthing simply means God is doing something new in you and taking you to the next level in Him. Birthing also means crossing over from one dimension to the next, which is something the enemy of souls does not want to happen; hence he will attack us. When Jesus was crossing over on the other side, there was a contrary wind that tried to kill the disciples. Recognize that in warfare, you will see, for example, different issues surface with family members – strife here, sickness there and other issues arise. But the enemy's real goal is to destroy the family. The plan of the enemy is often for you to focus on the little issues and miss the bigger picture of what he is really trying to do.

It is critical, during birthing, to know when the times and the seasons have changed; you cannot operate in summer the same way you operate in winter.

Always remember, when there is a birthing, you must choose your battles wisely, not every battle you should engage in. There are many weapons with which God wants us to fight during spiritual warfare, we must fight with the Blood of Jesus, we must fight with the Word of God, we must fight with our Praise and our Dance, we must fight with our Giving and there are times we will need to fight with Fasting and pull away from the crowd, so that our environment will change. We all want to have a better environment; if you are tired of your environment, you must begin to fight.

Stronghold/Strongman

Many times, people will get confused in terms of what is a stronghold and a strongman. Let us put it simply: a stronghold is a place that has been fortified so as to protect it against attack, a place where a particular cause or belief is strongly defined; it is an area dominating or occupied by a special group, a strongly fortified defense structure. People also enter a stronghold during a battle, but the definition we are speaking about is stronghold that comes against us according to 2 Corinthians 10. Your stronghold can be pride, fear, rejection, doubt, unbelief, infirmities among other things. For every stronghold there is a strongman which rules from the second heaven but the stronghold is over the person or within the person.

Demons always go back and forth, they cannot be everywhere at once (Matthew 18:18). Demons are connected by cords – spiritually speaking. We need to bind the strongman from over our lives and ask God to cut and cast off all connecting cords, any link, any order of command. (Psalm 2:3 and Psalm 129:4). Always remember that there are ruling spirits, unseen to the eyes, over your neighborhood, church, family, over individuals. We each need to look and see what negatives are happening in our community, for example, crime and violence. You need to see what the negative things are and understand why they are happening. You can change it by identifying what it is and begin to pray, as we have the authority for that change. Are divorces taking place in your family or community? Jesus showed us that before He could heal the blind man, he had to lead him out of the community. Every community has a different strongman and the people have different strongholds they are battling with. When demons gain entrance to the human body, they begin to establish different strongholds. People who live in certain communities and cities that are known for sexual sins, will most likely live that way because of the stronghold in that area.

It is therefore critical to carry out a spiritual mapping of an area before moving there to find out what strongholds are over that area. For example, what are the strongholds over California, Las Vegas, or New York? We need to identify that, because the strongman over the area is a reflection of the stronghold within the people.

Yokes

We must Fast to break the wicked schemes from nations that keep the people under oppression and bondage; because there are wicked people uniting globally with the intent of putting people in bondage. We must fast to break free, and to break the yoke.

In most countries that are benefiting from international lenders, most loans are tied to immorality, financial bondage, witchcraft, anti-Christ laws, and for this reason we must fast that God will undo heavy burden; to loose, to cut, to free, to deliver and to break all bonds.

Heavy taxation, economic stress, high interest rates and legal issues are some of the problems weighing down the people; and these are some of the things put in our way to block or curse us to stop us from advancing. They are heavy loads to carry.

Burdens and Oppression are demonic, oppressive spirits which instigate unjust laws and regulation, high price within the market place by companies.

Fasting breaks evil decrees, tears down ruling spirits over nations, lets the oppressed go free, breaks spiritual and physical forces of evil – especially countries that are ruled by socialism.

The Isaiah 58 Fast is a fast that breaks every oppression from nations and removes the bondage. This includes dictatorial leadership. This fast also breaks oppressive systems of government, wicked justice systems, generational strongholds, mind problems, fear and rejection, every other evil force is in place. When the people unite and fast, the Lord will move. Most global leaders, lead with demonic forces, which put the people under yoke and bondage. A yoke is anything that keeps you in bondage. A yoke is also wooden bars put across the neck of two animals to hold them together and it is used to put across a person's shoulder.

An unequal yoke occurs when a saved person is joined with an unsaved person together in covenant, for example, in marriage. It is as if a donkey and a cow joined together. They are going in 2 different directions and they are controlled by who instill the yoke.

Prayer and Fasting break yoke and bondage. Breaking means to separate or to become separated into 2 or more parts. For example, a 1 – 3-day fast will do the work.

When the enemy yokes us, he uses us, abuses us and oppresses us and he pulls us in any direction he wants. We need to be free from every yoke of oppression, every yoke of soul ties, every yoke of sexual uncleanness, addiction, sexual immorality, wrong relationship, drugs, witchcraft, video games, political organization, and also social network. We must break free.

We need also to break from any past unGodly agreements/covenants, as well as any legal rights to impose past agreements/contracts because we have the blood of Jesus Christ.

Chapter 24

UNDERSTANDING AND BREAKING THE BASTARD CURSE

Deuteronomy 23: 2 says, "One of illegitimate birth shall not enter the assembly of the Lord; even to the tenth generation none of his descendants shall enter the assembly of the Lord."

A "bastard" is defined "a person born of parents not married to each other; illegitimate child; anything inferior or varying from standard; (being) of illegitimate birth or of uncertain origin."

According to Deuteronomy 23: 2, the Bastard Curse is real. This curse has affected many nations and cultures, in particular the Black and Hispanic peoples, and it brings along with it rejection, bitterness, hatred, rebellion and lust. As a result, we see children being born out of wedlock (to unmarried parents), persons committing abortion and fathers who refuse to accept and embrace their children.

This curse will attack a lineage, and can also create great poverty within an entire nation. We have seen countries trying to pass laws in order to make the Bastard Curse seem unreal especially as it relates to inheritance, but the breaking of Spiritual laws is real;

and a nation or a community cannot be free until the Bastard Curse is broken. We must recognize, however, that this curse cannot be broken by way of the legal framework, but can only be rectified Spiritually and with Divine Intervention.

Most persons under the Bastard Curse find it difficult to get married or to have children without having the experience of a miscarriage. The Bastard Curse brings many negative experiences in families and nations; it increases crime and violence and causes great suffering. We need to begin to examine those on drugs and those involved in witchcraft, tattoos and prostitution to see their connection to the Bastard Curse. Furthermore, according to an article titled, "*The Consequences of Fatherlessness*", surveys have shown that "...children from fatherless homes are more likely to be poor, become involved in drug and alcohol abuse, drop out of school, and suffer from health and emotional problems. Boys are more likely to become involved in crime, and girls are more likely to become pregnant as teens." (Teachman, Jay D. "The Childhood Living Arrangements of Children and the Characteristics of Their Marriages." Journal of Family Issues 25 (January 2004): 86-111) These, in addition to many of the societal issues faced by countries today are often the result of the Bastard Curse. (2 Samuel 11: 2 – 5).

When a child is conceived through adultery, it opens the door for incest, murder, rape, conspiracy and pain, and can follow up to ten generations. Look at what happened to King David's administration, his children and family, as a result of the adultery he committed.

The Church is not exempt from the effects of the Bastard Curse, because it affects church growth and causes instability. There are many persons who constantly change churches, unable to settle down. If you should check the information, they were born out of wedlock and were rejected by their fathers, whether spiritual or biological.

Another issue that stems from the Bastard Curse is Abortion, and it is not only about the voluntary or involuntary termination of physical pregnancies, but on a deeper level, it includes the termination of an individual or nation's purpose.

The Moabites, from whose lineage Ruth came, were conceived through incest which brought a Bastard Curse. But through Jesus Christ, God redeemed us from the curse of the law. Just as He did through Jabez, God used Ruth to show, that regardless of whatever the curse - bastard or any other - Jesus Christ will break that curse when we accept Him.

In light of all this, we need to begin educating our children about the dangers of sex out of marriage or having children out of wedlock, the danger of Incest and Abortion. All of these open the door for the Bastard Curse. Jesus Christ wants to destroy that curse that has been robbing communities and nations. If you check our prison population, approximately 70 % of those within the prisons were raised with no fathers in their lives because of the Bastard Curse. It is time for us to destroy that curse so that the next generation may be free from the struggles and the pain and suffering. We must pray aggressively for this curse to be broken.

Chapter 25

THE FOURTH WATCH FOR BREAKTHROUGH PRAYER

Timing is critical to the effectiveness of our prayers in an effort to get results. Originally, in the Bible the Hebrews had three watches but the Romans extended it to four. There is a fourth watch that is mentioned within the Bible to wrestle with God for breakthrough. They are:

First Watch   6 p.m. – 9 p.m.

Second Watch   9 p.m. – 12 a.m.

Third Watch   12 a.m. – 3 a.m.

Fourth Watch   3 a.m. – 6 a.m.

The Fourth Watch is the time God wants us to rise with prayer and power to pray and God will open portals. During this time, there is a manifestation of angelic activities within the earth. There are several scriptures about the Third and Fourth watch that prove the importance.

1. In Genesis 32: 22 -31, it was during that time of the Fourth Watch that Jacob struggled with God for his breakthrough; he wrestled for the promise, he wrestled for the breakthrough, he wrestled for answers, for the glory of God, and he wrestled for a deeper realm and revelation of the spirit. When we wrestle in prayer during that time, character transformation takes place, our enemies will be eliminated, God will give us tactics and strategy during that time, supernatural intervention, revival and a time to recover from the enemy.

2. Moses led the children of Israel through the Red Sea during the fourth watch and God destroyed the Egyptians and took off their chariot wheels (Exodus 14: 24 - 26). So, when we pray within the Fourth watch, God begins to fight for us. It came to pass, that in the morning watch, the Lord looked to the host of the Egyptians through the pillar of fire and cloud and troubled the host of the Egyptians – Exodus 14: 24.

3. Gideon, also, defeated the Midianite during the Fourth Watch (Judges 7: 19 - 24)

4. In Matthew 25:1-13 there were 5 wise and 5 foolish operating during a certain watch and at midnight there was a cry.

5. Peter and Jesus walked on water during the fourth watch (Matthew 14: 25 - 26). So, praying during the Fourth Watch allows us to walk in the supernatural, deal with contrary wind and demonic attack and cross over - stepping out of the boat, meaning to step out in faith, going to the next level. These are benefits to praying in the Fourth Watch.

6. Jesus was raised from the dead during the Fourth Watch (Matthew 28: 1 and Luke 2: 8 - 14). There may be things in our lives that seems dead, by praying in the Fourth Watch things will begin to resurrect.

7. Luke 12: 35 - 40 shows the evidence of the different watches, we see the Second and Third. Take note at verse 38, this shows the importance of the Watch.

What if all Christians begin to pray around the different watches? We would have great change.

As in the book of Job, we must command the morning to bring forth blessing. Job 38: 12 says "Have you commanded the morning since your days began, and caused the dawn to know its place," God wants us to pray that the things that the enemy planted against us daily will be cancelled out.

Matthew 13: 24 - 25 shows us that while men slept, the enemy came and sowed tares among the wheat and went his way. So, when we command the morning to bring forth blessing and cancel out every plan the enemy has against you, you get the victory.

Remember every good seed planted in the field by God's people, the enemy will always want to sow tares to destroy the good seeds that we planted. We want to ensure that the good wheat comes forth and the bad tares are destroyed. The Fourth Watch brings forth our harvest and cancels the plans of the enemy. It is time for us to pray that God will gather and burn up all the tares that the enemy plants against your good work, your marriage, your church, your finances. Tares can be negative speech, gossip, lies, witchcraft, undermined, sabotage, and other evils. While we want good and positive things to take place in our lives, remember both tares and wheat look alike, so sometimes you will not know what is in your midst until you begin to pray. What if the enemy is camouflaged as a friend? We will have to pray for exposure. Not every Israelite is a true Israelite. How do you distinguish a Christian? "By their fruit you will know them" Jesus said. (Matthew 7:15-20). As we pray, God will begin to send forth His angels to begin to uproot what needs to be uprooted and preserve what needs to be preserved. We cannot do it ourselves, only God can do the separation. Remember wheat and tares resemble each other, so it is hard to discern at times.

Only Fasting and Prayer brings the necessary exposure. It is time for us to begin to watch. We have seen the Watches mentioned over 24 times in the New Testament.

In Mark 13: 33-37, Jesus outlined that we should watch and pray, we must be alert, we must occupy all the different Watches. Also read Psalm 119: 148, Psalm 63: 6, and also Psalm 90: 4.

God is calling back to the Kingdom to take back the Watch Tower, so it is critical for us to understand the different Watches. All are effective but I believe that the Fourth Watch 3 a.m. to 6 a.m. is more effective against the kingdom of darkness.

Chapter 26

THE KEYS OF THE KINGDOM

Keys give us access, to open doors – doors of opportunity granting us authority in an area so that we may enter into greatness. There are portals/doorways of knowledge, mystery, power and wisdom all of which are keys to great things, which also come with Divine grace and favor. We cannot enter any door – naturally or spiritually – without keys.

When someone has a key, they have the authority to open and close that door. God gave Peter the keys of the kingdom of heaven which gives power to forbid or to allow, to bind and to loose! God has to trust us before He can give us keys. Keys should always be used properly; they must be used responsibly, because keys control access - not only to let us in and out - but also allows us to deny access to anything that would work contrary to the fulfillment of our purpose.

Matthew 6 teaches us about the keys within the prayer that everyone should pray daily. The apostles asked Jesus to teach them to pray effectively to manifest the kingdom. Pray to the Father, pray without distraction, and do not pray to be seen by men. When you pray in secret, He will reward you openly, pray simply. This is the format that Jesus gave us when we are praying regarding the Kingdom.

When we pray, we are to declare the Holiness of God; declare Who He is – His majesty and power; we ought to praise and bless His name for His holiness! Each name represents each of His characteristics; His Presence is sacred. When His Kingdom comes, His will, *shall* be done, and what takes place in heaven, must take place in the earth, because that is Kingdom Alignment; it facilitates established Kingdom rules in our lives, in our ministry, in our nation and we need them to come down. (Luke 4: 18-19, Mark 16)

Healing the sick, Preaching the Gospel, Deliverance, Manifestation of God's Power - these are some of the Kingdom Keys that God wants to manifest through us, to deal with our needs, and bring to our lives those things allotted to us daily – spiritually and physically. We must ask for what we need.

Remember, ask the Lord for the things that make us better able to carry out God's work. Ask Him for grace and favor. Remember prayer for our needs must connect to Kingdom concerns - Forgiveness, Debt Write-offs – nothing must have us in bondage. We must owe no man but love, we must ask the Lord to strengthen us to stand strong, that we will overcome all evil and temptation, we will rise from the wilderness, we will walk in God's ways and God's will. We will walk in humility, we will not fall for fame, sex, money, prosperity, and nothing will allow us to fall away. When we pray, we must remember that all power belongs to God, and that He can give us power. He is the Supreme Being, all things are created by Him, for Him and through Him.

Chapter 27

PRAY FOR CLIMATE CHANGE IN AMERICA

The posture of a nation is a reflection of the Church. The negative happenings that are taking place in America for example racism, classism, rampant sexual immorality and even inhumane treatment of illegal aliens is a result of the Church falling asleep. We have seen sins of many kinds taking over the Church in the United States of America (U.S.A.).

The U.S.A. is very important to God's plan; the blessing that God has been pouring out on the U.S.A. is mainly because of the humanitarian work they have been doing over the years, the different countries they have helped and the spreading of the gospel that America has been doing. There is no country in the world that has done more than the U.S.A. regarding advancing the Kingdom of God in terms of help through funding and humanitarian efforts - they are Number One. They have been sending missionaries throughout the World, and they have extended great help to the Jews – taking many in where other nations have rejected them. The enemy knows that, which is why he is working overtime in his efforts to destroy the U.S.A. This is why the Church needs to open their eyes and discern to see what is happening.

Instead of liberals and conservatives blaming each other, they should see who the real enemy is. That is why God is calling the Church within the U.S.A. and other countries that have benefited from them to pray that God will raise up the Josephs, the Daniels, and the Nehemiahs that will rebuild the nations by re-establishing and rebuilding the altar. When there was a famine in the book of Kings, when and where Jezebel had turned the people to worship Baal, Elijah first had to rebuild the altar before he called the fire. It is time to rebuild the altar in America and call down the fire. Prayer changes things! It brings supernatural intervention, changes the environment, and it exposes falsehood and brings truth. There are different prayers that are Scriptural and in the Bible.

1. **Prayer of Thanksgiving/Blessing** where we thank God for His goodness, what He has done for us and what He is about to do. Luke 11:2-4 Matthew 6:9-13

2. **Prayer of Petition** we see this in the Bible with Hannah, Esther and Daniel who all made petitions to God.

3. **Intercessory Prayer** simply means praying on behalf of others. 1 Timothy 2: 1 and Ephesians 6. Intercessory prayers also include warfare, where we can bind and loose.

4. **Supplication**, which is asking for one's self. (Philippians 4: 6) Remember Intercessory Prayers are for others, Supplication is for us – it is a request for help for our daily needs. We all have needs, so we have to make supplication.

5. **Corporate/Public Prayer.** We see this in the book of Acts (Acts 13:1-3, Acts 6:1-6) even when they were choosing leaders, in order not to make mistakes they would go into corporate and public prayer.

6. **Closet Prayer**, which is our devotion, where we pray secretly. Matthew 6:5-6

7. **The Prayer of Faith** is exemplified in James 5:15 and 1 John 5:14, and happens when we pray for the sick. In such prayers, we can use a point of contact.

God also has been speaking to me over the years about the midday and midnight prayer and how effective it is to destroy Satan's kingdom. When you pray, pray simply according to Matthew 6, pray from your heart, and do not pray with empty words or vain repetition or a long prayer that brings confusion.

Avoid distraction when you are praying. Never pray to attack someone else, we must always pray and ask

God to establish His rule and His will to take place in the earth.

1. Pray for physical needs which is totally linked to Kingdom rule and Kingdom concern.

2. Pray for forgiveness, both God to forgive us and we forgive others.

3. Pray that God will lead us not into temptation and deliver us from evil. Matthew 6, which is referred to as the Disciple's Prayer is a prayer that every Christian should pray on a daily basis because there are blessings and benefits, we receive.

We must pray for debt cancelation and debt write-off, debt forgiveness which includes waiver and bail out. There are many large organizations that have been receiving bailout while the poor has not been getting that benefit. We have to pray for a fair distribution of resources to take place in the earth. There is no shortage of resources. The resources are in the wrong hands and are being distributed among the wrong people. That is why as Kingdom people we have to begin to pray again.

Ephesians 6:18 says, <u>"Praying always with all prayer and supplication in the Spirit, being watchful to this</u>

end with all perseverance and supplication for all the saints."

God wants us to pray in the Spirit also. When we pray in the Spirit, we pray accurately. We pray God's will according to Romans 8: 26 – 27.

The focus of Spiritual Warfare is to open doors, personally and Kingdom-wise. (Colossians 4: 3, 1 Corinthians 16: 9). We must pray that the Ministry of the Gospel may advance and that utterance may be given to God's servants that they may open their mouths boldly, that God will allow His Apostles to make known the mystery of the Gospel.

We must pray that God will break the chains from all His ambassadors. Chains are anything that the enemy uses to limit us from advancing. For example, most countries are putting in travel restrictions to hinder the Apostles or Five-Fold Ministry from advancing into certain regions and this includes harsh immigration policies, and other legal ramifications. That is why the Bible says Prayer stops the enemy's plan: it changes the direction of a nation, it brings healing, it breaks drought, it causes earthquakes, it brings prison breaks - when they prayed the building shook! (Acts 2 and Acts 4). Prayer brings Climate Change!

Prayer Points

When praying for the U.S.A., pray for the following that:

1. God will open the eyes of the people to see the true enemies of America.

2. Raise up new and righteous advisors to surround leaders at all levels.

3. The U.S.A. will return to God fully.

4. Pride and Arrogance will be broken.

5. Mercy and Compassion will be restored for the fatherless, the voiceless, the immigrants.

6. The Church will be awakened and holiness will return to the Church

7. New politicians will rise with the Joseph, Daniel and Nehemiah anointings.

8. The Spirit of Jezebel will be broken from the nation.

9. The Spirits of Racism and Classism will be broken and the Spirit of Grace and Supplication will be poured out.

10. There will be protection of the Constitution.

11. Family will be the First Line of Government and finance will be given for community empowerment.

12. The Spiritual walls and gates will be rebuilt as in the book of Nehemiah.

13. More missionaries will rise up from the U.S.A. and help other nations, so that Jesus Christ will be Lord over the U.S.A. and no other gods.

Chapter 28

CHANGE BRINGS CHANGE

Everybody is crying out for change and are debating what kind of change they want to see. Some talk of political change, others talk about change in the marketplace, some talk about individual changes in their lives – new personal resolutions and goals; still others talk about Climate Change – all kinds of changes. Over the past 10 years we have seen a lot of changes taking place, but most of them are negative. What was once considered despicable has now become "honorable". The poor are forgotten more and more as the years go by as compassion and care lessen with time. The global priorities have been turned upside down and we are heading down a dangerous path; even those coming on the scene talking of change come mainly with deception. The only true positive changes that have remained and will continue to remain truly positive are the changes that take place of heart, mind and lifestyle. Further to that, our motives - the way we think and how we function on a daily basis -affect our very environment. Regardless of how much we talk about Climate Change, we will only see the Climate Change we are looking for when Man begins to change. If we keep doing the same negative thing, how can we get positive change?

Irrespective of what plans, goals and objectives we have – personal, national or global – if our lifestyle, mindset and heart remain the same, we will not get the positive results we are seeking.

Fostering Positive Change

Oftentimes we hear people complain that politicians are not doing anything and that they want better. But how will they get better if they themselves remain the same – having the same heart, same mind, the same lifestyle? They do not attract better because they choose to remain the same. Likewise, people say they want a society without God - why do they complain when crime, violence and shooting takes place? We all want better security forces within our nation. But how can we expect better, when the government maintains low wages for security personnel and neglects the people? The society we create is the society will get. When we build from the blueprint of other nations or with the plans of others, then we will face what they face and get their "plagues" in addition to our own internal issues. We do not need another wall, we do not need bigger walls, we do not need more prisons, we do not need Biometric systems, we do not need Radio Frequency Identification (RFIDs) – we need a heart, mind and lifestyle change. Implementing a system without God does not stop corruption – all we are doing is passing the plate of corruption to different hands. We embrace the same system being passed on to friends and opportunists to continue sharing from the same plate of corruption and no true and positive change happens.

Oftentimes people create "new" systems to deal with the problems, but all they are doing is neglecting the real issue to be dealt with and ignoring the real solutions. What happens when a person who is broke and in debt, continues to do nothing to change it while expecting the change? They will remain in debt while the situation worsens. There are even pastors who want their church to change, but remain with the same mindset and the same way of doing business. Such persons can make all the declarations they want to make, if they do not change their mindset and how they do things, everything will remain the same.

Self-Evaluation

Every person now has to evaluate him/herself. Everyone must remember that however we treat others, so shall we be treated – what you sow you will reap. We do not believe in karma; we believe in Retribution and Seedtime and Harvest.

Many people have used the power, grace and favor that God has given to them to negatively impact the lives of others. Many are on the street now without food. What are you willing to change as you come to the close of the year in order to see a positive change in the year ahead? You have the answer.

Chapter 29

GOD STILL SPEAKS

God has been speaking from the time of creation until today. He speaks through His servants and when Man refuses to listen to God's servants, then Man pays the price. We have been destroying the planet for the sake of greed – greedy organizations who influence nations and politicians to pass unjust laws which impact and affect us all, particularly the poor, the fatherless, and the voiceless, within a nation.

The number one threat to the planet is not Global Warming or Climate Change - it is Sin. Sin affects everything from the Climate to the animals to us human beings, especially as we consume the very same animals. (Read the Book of Genesis)

Scientists will now become bankrupt of ideas and answers because they no longer acknowledge God as the Creator. Many are now worshipping the creation without realizing that the creation depends on God for sustenance and relevance of purpose (Psalms 148)

It is critical for different leaders and lawmakers to come together to develop a plan which could be driven by the United Nations to help save lives and deal with other disasters which could be coming.

Take a look at several prophecies from Part 3 of the Word of the Lord given to us at Restoration World Outreach Ministries Incorporated, published in The Gleaner (Jamaica) in 2018.

#2 Focus on Revelation 5, Revelation 8, and Revelation 18. We are going to see a lot of problems with the cosmos (cosmic convulsions) similar to Exodus 10: 21 – as a sign of God's displeasure in the Earth. There will be a lot of activity on/with the sun, and scientists will have their hands full. There will be problems with vegetation as well as volcanic eruptions, increase of earthquakes in diverse places, and serious problems with marine life. Many fish will die and there will be great pollution. Meteors will fall and there will be increased testing of weapons in the sea. (Joel 2: 30 – 32, Jeremiah 9: 15 – 23). All these things will affect crop, property, and life. We will be seeing greater flooding, more bloodshed, and pestilence.

#7 There will be wars in the ocean. Many problems will arise in the oceans, which can cause major losses, especially with tuna fish. Many who eat tuna fish will get sick because of ocean contamination.

#16 Nations need to be ready to assist other nations because a chemical disaster is at large. Many seas are going to be polluted due to rebellion in Man throughout the ecosystem. I saw in the Spirit the extinction of Dolphins due to severe pollution. Due to the severe pollution that will be taking place, many will become infected from every class level. However, the poor will be more susceptible to the health hazards.

#19 Fires will burn in diverse places in America, Africa, and west of Indonesia.

#26 We will see cyber-electronic devices, IDs, and other data-driven systems that will be implemented under the guise of boosting national security and bringing economic growth to countries, but the Lord tells His people to be ready.

(Read also numbers 15,17, 19, 33 and 34.)

Signs Of Times

Luke 21: 25 says, "And there will be signs in the sun, in the moon, and in the stars; and on the earth distress of nations, with perplexity, the sea and the waves roaring;"

We are seeing these six (6) occurrences taking place in the earth like never before.

We have seen the devastation caused by fires, in different parts of the United States – California, the

Carolina as well as volcanic eruptions in Hawaii and other parts of the world; as well as earthquakes in Indonesia with death toll of 300 and rising. There is even a major disaster in Florida as was prophesied – they call it the Red Tide; Dolphins, sharks and other marine life are perishing in alarming numbers and are being washed up on the shores. Scientists say the worst is to come. All this is having a negative impact on marine life as well as human consumption and economic growth. The questions we need to ask are, "Is the consumption of fish still safe?", "Is our water system still safe for human consumption?" "Is there additional testing to ensure that there is no further disease breakout?" and "How safe and stable is our communication system, are we ready for a blackout"

While many talk about Global Warming, the greatest hindrance to the environment are Human Beings. Our own actions have been destroying our environment. Weapons testing and polluting the ocean for economic gain. Scientists also have gone beyond their human boundaries and some of what they are doing is impacting negatively on the environment. We are now seeing an increase in "freak" occurrences such as freak storms and flash floods.

In Genoa, Italy on August 14, 2018, strong winds caused a raised highway to collapse killing at least 25 and injuring 11 pulled from the rubble – according to Genoa's Mayor Marco Bucci.

Further to that, on August 8, 2018, a rare fire tornado was reported in the United Kingdom appropriately referred to it as a "firenado." Firefighters in Derbyshire, England, captured a strange and frightening natural phenomenon on video.

Chapter 30

PARENTS, EXERCISE YOUR RIGHTS! CHANGE THE CLIMATE FOR THE YOUTH

The rights of parents are coming under attack. There are international stakeholders that want to diminish the rights of parents. It is critical for parents to know the God-given rights and authority they have as parents and that they are responsible for that and are accountable to God. God also warned in His word that the type of parenting one displays can determine the life span of a parent on earth. (Deuteronomy 11: 19 – 21; Deuteronomy 6: 7 and Proverbs 22: 6). There are even specific terminologies and meanings that people want to change in order to facilitate and support their diabolical plans to rob parents of their parental rights and authorities.

What Parents Can Do

First and foremost, you cannot be an effective parent without God's help.

Always set an example that your children can follow. They do what we do.

Always be vigilant and look for signs of abuse and depression, and even bullying at school. As soon as you identify these signs, you need to seek help, especially since there are a number of students today contemplating suicide. Part of this comes from the exposure they are getting to things like marijuana, immoral activities – some get pressured by all sexes. So it is critical to pray the Word of God over them daily.

As parents, you must always create a climate for open dialogue – where there can be dialogue without fear to address their problems. Also, ensure that the climate that exists within your home will not negatively affect them to the point that they want to run away from home.

Do Not Compromise

1. Never compromise with your children. Remember that you are their parent, not their friend.

2. Parents must always know the whereabouts of their children and know their friends as well. Spend less time on social media and use that time to bond with your children.

3. Get involved with the Parent Teachers' Association and do spot checks on their curriculum so you know what they are being taught.

4. Parents, do not be afraid to hug your children – especially the boys; and speak life and the fulfillment of their purpose over them every day.

5. Never try to make your children into what you want to be; let them be whom God has said they are to be.

6. Always seek God for the name of your child, and how to grow them with regard to their purpose. Teach them about morals, values, how to dress, etc. The world has more than enough half-naked people running around and does not need any more. Remind them that everything on or in this earth that is precious is always covered.

7. Teach your children about the fact that God made them perfect – so they do not need to "bleach", darken, tattoo, pierce various body parts or anything of that nature because they were made well.

8. Teach them about the power of submission and how it is for their protection more than anything else.

9. As parents, you must lead by example, and whatever you expect of them must begin with you first. Never teach them hate, teach them the power of Forgiveness. Teach them the Word of God and how to pray and to stay away from witchcraft and any other things that are not the principles and the instructions of God.

10. Never "poison" your children against another person – especially the other parent.

11. Teach them to respect the Law, their elders, others within the society and themselves and to stay away from alcoholic beverages and gambling.

12. Teach them (both male and female) to cook, clean and be entrepreneurial in their endeavors.

13. Teach them how to join (and stay in) a line and how to be patriotic and to respect the flag and how to say "Yes ma'am" or "No Sir" when addressing other adults/elders.

14. Never discipline them when you are angry, and always explain to them the purpose of Discipline.

Parents, remember, 90% of the problems in society has its roots in the home. You are the first line of authority. You are preparing leaders, husbands, wives and whatever you do is impacting the society. The institution of Family today is broken and if we are going to bring change to that and ultimately to the society, then it must begin in the home.

Know your rights and exercise them. Otherwise, then very shortly you will have no rights.

Stand In The Gap For The Next Generation

Ezekiel 22: 30 says, "So I sought for a man among them who would make a wall, and stand in the gap before Me on behalf of the land, that I should not destroy it; but I found no one."

Many times, people will criticize the Church and ask what they are doing about the negative happenings within a nation or the world. But we must recognize that we are the Church – every profession – and we have a responsibility individually and collectively, to stand in the gap for nations. We have become a nation of people that have become caught up in our own little issues/problems/situations forgetting that we also have a duty to each other and to our nation. Some are so caught up in showing off their latest 'self-improvement' projects – who has the latest clothes or enhanced body parts – and when tragedy strikes that is when they get concerned.

When negative happenings begin – Murder, Rape and Famine and then Hopelessness sets in, it means that there is a break/breach within the spiritual walls of the nation. If someone breaks into a home, if the owner simply adds a burglar alarm without fixing the breach – the broken window/door – then their efforts are wasted. Hence, God wants persons of every profession at every level to make themselves available to Him to be used to rebuild the walls – not the physical, but spiritual walls. We need to 'Stand in the Gap'.

Standing in the gap is a metaphor for committed intercession. When there is a gap between Man and God, someone needs to stand in and intercede so that God can repair the breach for us. Hence, we have a responsibility to first identify the breach in every profession and stand in.

When there is a breach in the walls everything comes in – anything takes place. So, if we are looking for restoration of the family, a good justice system, good governance and healing within a nation, then it is the responsibility of everyone to stand in the gap that the spiritual barriers will be rebuilt. Regardless of the systems or laws put in place, no change will come if there is a gap in the wall.

Every Profession

In order to be effective, every profession knows its own terminologies and jargon and so, knows the precise words to use as opposed to the ordinary lay person who would not be as knowledgeable in that area. For example, a lawyer knows the jargon and terms that he/she would use for certain matters, like 'petition', 'counter-petition' 'recuse', 'abrogate' so they could pray accordingly employing those terms that John Q. Public would not ordinarily know. A person who deals with the economy of a nation needs to stand in the gap for the things that of that industry that are affecting the nation – inflation, devaluation of the dollar, fiscal policies and so on. They know the terminologies to use as they pray to stop the negative and ask for the increase of the positive. Doctors would know the diseases that are plaguing the nation and would pray accordingly for them to stop using medical terminologies. They would stand in the gap to minimize sicknesses and diseases that are eating away the nation – cancer, HIV, and others and that God will release medical breakthroughs to heal the nation. Security forces also need to stand in the gap - they simply cannot focus on the physical, but also the spiritual aspect.

Interestingly, there is a name of God – a name ascribed to God which represents every one of these industries in our society.

Effective intercession brings change within a nation, but each person who stands in the gap must realize that we cannot operate the same way that we operated 20 years ago. 20 years ago, we did not have the technological revolution we now have and now as knowledge has increased, so has the technological warfare. There are now games and software that are designed to pollute the minds of our youth and encourage them to commit crimes and do other things; and this is a breach. We need people to rise up in the Information Technology arena to use the relevant jargon and references as they stand in the gap and fight for our young people and the future of the nation.

Recognize that the mind and eyes are direct links to the soul and as such whoever will control the mind and eyes will control the next generation.

It is the responsibility of every profession to stand in the gap so that change will take place.

Chapter 31

PRAYER, THE PEN AND GUNS

Many of the issues being faced worldwide throughout the various nations are the result of Selfishness – putting 'self' first in very key areas when it ought not to be so.

Many times people try to blame others for problems they created/allowed in the first instance – crime, violence – but continually ignore their role in making it happen. People solely blame those who carry the guns, but ignore the serious destruction and damage done by those with the pen! Those with the pen make covenants and sign contracts – contracts to kill others, contracts to do serious damage of great significance!

There are many in positions of influence who pay some to put pen to paper to the ruination of many others. There is a movie called 'House of Cards', which truly reveals such inner workings!

A person may not physically hold the gun and pull the trigger, but there are those who use the pen to approve actions, tell lies and distort facts, they are just as guilty of murder, if not, more than those who do the deed! Furthermore, those who pass laws and write or sign approve statements, write songs, movies that exploit our children and their fragile bodies are just as guilty as those who literally defile, abuse or rape them.

Many of us want to see crime and violence reduced, but what about the intangible damage being done that cannot be easily fixed/remedied?

Prayer Reveals Ourselves To Us

Many will criticize prayer and make efforts to expel it from society. Others will try to inject everything except prayer to the True and Living God into our daily lives. But what we must recognize is that as we pray, prayer reveals our hearts and our motives to us; and we need that if we are going to improve and grow personally, and if we are going to bring solutions to the table! Prayer does not help God - it helps us - and it changes us for the better if we are willing to yield. Prayer opens our eyes to discern truth, light and darkness. Prayer renews our minds to see things differently and to see the way God wants us to see.

The world is more interested in treating symptoms than curing the root issue, because treating brings greater profit. They do not care if a few people die in the process! Every man has a God-given, kingly path within him, so it is inherent within him to have dominion. However, to dominate and conquer without Divine direction is the order of the day, and to our detriment. We must walk in dominion, but it must be done God's way!

In addition to this, everyone wants to be upfront; no one wants to be in the middle or at the back. We continue to research, talk philosophies in an effort to determine why people engage in crime and violence, without realizing that the answer to that 'elusive' question has already been documented in the Bible (Jeremiah 17: 9; Matthew 15: 18 – 19). Why waste money re-inventing the wheel?

Every New Year, people make New Year's resolutions about making changes so that they may see change, but they refuse to change or are not consistent in their actions, and as a result there are no real changes.

Sometimes God allows change to come through the introduction of harsh economic measures, famine and when the people realize and cry out, then will God send a deliverer. So regardless of the political leaders elected to office, the cycle remains the same until they change.

Interestingly, Man always tries to avoid the things that always brings the right change to him. The Bible brings positive change, Man avoids it! Prayer brings change, Man bans it! All the enemy does is re-brand and re-package inferior products and calls it transformation.

Recognize that Prayer allows God's will to take place in your life, family and your nation; and it allows heaven and earth to align in agreement. It keeps us from falling into temptation; it allows us to hear God's voice.

If leaders were praying and listening to God's voice before making decisions, could you imagine how different things would be right now?

Luke 18: 1 says: "Then He spoke a parable to them, that men always ought to pray and not lose heart,"

Furthermore, and finally, Philippians 4: 6 says, "Be anxious for nothing, but in everything by prayer and supplication, with thanksgiving, let your requests be made known to God..."

Chapter 32

WHY PEOPLE GENERALLY HATE THE TRUTH

Have you ever noticed that when people hear the truth they kick, scream, throw a tantrum or blatantly refute it?

People hate truth because it causes them to look at themselves and lets them realize that how they view themselves and what really is are very different. Furthermore, truth reveals deep things – even hidden things, and so it brings things in the dark to light. When there is no light in someone, they hate anything that will bring what is in the dark to light.

Regardless of the breakthrough we need to happen in our society – whether economic, political or security-related – we will never get that breakthrough until we deal with the truth.

Oftentimes people will say they need female leaders because the men have failed. But while God uses both genders, having a female leader will not change anything if foundational truths are not addressed and change is not executed. Only truth can free us from deception and bondage. (John 8: 32)

Why does fake news sell but truth is always hidden? It is so in traditional media as well as on social media –

the truth is always played down. Truth is not to be hidden. When you do, it will swim like oil on water. For example, the Abortion debate, where it is being stated that women are free to do whatever they want to do with their bodies, it is not so! Your body is the temple of the Holy Spirit. Our bodies are to glorify God – He owns our bodies. Our bodies are not cemeteries, and we are accountable to God for what we do in our bodies. Most of the things that negatively affect us – physically or spiritually – is the result of what we do in/with our bodies.

There are many who will capitalize on the mistakes we make with our bodies – doctors, politicians, bosses – but you are the ones who will pay for it, and so will your children and their children. This opens the door to the enemy's attacks and gives the devil what is called Legal Rights.

Truths

Regarding the notion that "Truth is what you make it," we might ask: if truth is merely a social construct, then what can you say to a society that encourages raping and murdering women, or tolerates the sexual abuse of children? If their truths allow them those actions, on what ground can you declare such practices to be wrong? And, on what basis does another nation give a global outcry to say it is wrong/abusive/inhumane – where does the truth lie?

Many truths are presented out there, but in fact, there is only one Spirit of Truth. The Holy Spirit brings us to all Truth and the Bible is the guide which gives us joy, life, healing and direction. (John 16: 3; 2 Timothy 3: 16 - 17) When we reject the truth, the Lord has to allow adversity so that we will see truth in action. So, when Man says God does not heal, He will allow situations to occur where you will need healing. Additionally, the debate on Climate Change or problems in the cosmos, were already clearly stated in Daniel, Revelation and the latter part of the Psalms.

Many ask why they should believe the Bible, because Man wrote the Bible. But who wrote all the scientific books that we embrace as truth?

If we say that "Truth is what science tells us," then that would mean that only scientific statements are meaningful. If that is so, then logically, it would mean that the very statement (and belief) that only scientific statements are meaningful would be self-condemning and absolutely meaningless, since such a statement is philosophical and not scientific.

Out of God comes the very word Science as we speak of His Omniscience. So neither science nor its principles could exist without God.

Do you realize that every profession that exists is connected to the study of God's creation? Read Psalm 111: 2 – 3.

Only the truth of God can sanctify us and it is His Word which is Truth. He is the only solution for the global issues and give us peace. Everything else is counterfeit.

Chapter 33

PRAYER CAN CHANGE YOUR CLIMATE

There are many scriptures in the Bible that have a positive effect on Climate Change. There are also scriptures that discuss poverty within a nation. Many mock Prayer not realizing that prayer will be the only solution in the End Time that will have a positive outcome on Climate Change.

Many disasters are happening globally, disasters beyond the norm. We also see storms and hurricanes occurring beyond the normal season. All these happenings will baffle scientists. In order to experience a positive outcome on Climate Change, we need to pray.

It is now very important how, what and to Whom we pray. Many gods exist but there is only one Almighty God - we must be careful not to pray to the creation but only pray to the Creator. There are many praying to the universe and this is bringing poverty on Mankind.

In James 5: 17 – 18, the prophet prayed and his prayer brought positive Climate Change and it impacted the entire nation. For three years there was no rain which brought famine and drought on the land. Most of the people began to worship Baal, the god of prosperity, the prophet first had to rebuild the altars that were broken down, then he called the fire which would bring sanctification, bring back the zeal and the passion for the people to turn from idols and return to the true and living God. When nations truly pray and repent, it will break famine and drought and bring spiritual and physical rain. (1 Kings 19: 41 - 42) This shows the importance of prayer and how it impacts the climate.

Intensity in Intercession will bring change. Persistence in Intercession will bring Climate Change. Luke 11: 6 - 13 shows us that prayer changes the atmosphere and breaks the cloud, we also see it in the Book of Joel where the nation was going through drought and disaster. Agriculture and Farming in general were affected; Man was affected, animals were affected, but God instructed the priest and the people to lead the change in repentance and along with the government. This stopped the disaster.

When a nation is going through drought, famine, crime/violence and lack of vision, the first thing to do is to pray persistently in Intercession. The book of Jonah also shows us the goodness of God. Demonic influences will negatively impact the atmosphere or climate. We see this take place in the books of Genesis and Exodus – how the sins of Man negatively impacted the environment and that is why we need atonement for change.

The sins of Man can alter and change God's original plan within the earth. Once there was no rain but there was only mist that watered the earth; but because of Man's sin, that was altered and the environment was changed.

In each territory and nation that is experiencing famine, the people have the power of prayer to change the negative happenings within their nation, even over our personal lives we can determine what takes place. We have the authority to determine what climate we want to embrace. The power of prayer opens the heavens. Prayer breaks stronghold over our lives, over our nation, over our city. God created the earth perfectly but it is Man's lifestyle that brought negative impact on the earth. Change in laws will not change the climate, what we need is a change of heart. When our heart changes, our speech will change and our mind will change. The breaking down of family impacts the climate. There are many that are rebelling against God. The family should begin to pray for unity and a prosperous environment. When a united family prays there is change. Over 13 million persons are hungry because of climate activity.

Climate Change and Man's Ways

To see our planet, go beyond the perception of what Man calls Climate Change, the number one cause is sin against God. Sin is the number one cause for climate change. Social injustice causes climate change. Greed, negative happenings, Man trying to legislate God out of the globe and Man worshiping idols, Man stopping God's word from being declared in the environment.

Hebrews 11 speaks to us that everything was created by God's Word. It says, <u>"By faith we understand that the worlds were framed by the word of God, so that the things which are seen were not made of things which are visible."</u> According to Genesis 1, everything was created by God's word – including the climate. So, the question is, when damage takes place in the environment through Man's sinful ways, what then would we use to repair the damage? Furthermore, the word *"frame"* means to *"set in order, adjust, complete what is lacking, make fully ready, mending and repair."*

Real Change Required

Regardless of political speeches, money is wasted to promote a Climate Change Agenda, while people are starving, while people are sinning against God, we will always have climate issues, and there will be no change until we embrace the change we truly need to make.   Man and Man's actions determine what takes place within the earth.

In order to save our planet, we need to begin to change our ways and our direction.   An unprecedented change has to take place, new heart, new mind, new spirit – a repenting heart. We need to have a broader view of Climate Change.   If Jonah could fast and the impact of the fast can birth the judgement of God on a nation, we can do the same also, we can fast.   If Elijah could change through prayer and intercession the entire economic system within a nation, we can make that change; we can stop earthquakes, tsunamis, tornadoes, and disasters within nations, through prayer and repentance.

I believe that if nations continue to persecute the Church, shut down churches, pass laws to minimize public worship, then we will see disasters like never before. This will show us that the Word of God, the Presence of God, the Blood of Jesus, God's Promises, Prayer, Praise, Worship, and Dancing will be key in the End Time to create a healthy environment. There are companies which are putting policies in place to take worship out of the work place – including many long-standing companies.   We are about to see many of them crash to the ground.

In Numbers 21, there was no water; there was dryness and no food. The people were suffering from self-inflicting punishment resulting from their action. Healing comes from looking to Christ. Many of the people were discouraged. Positive words cure a dry season, it opens wells of water. His word creates new environment, new resources. Praise causes water to flow from wells. God instructed the people to unite and gather together and sing *"Spring up, O well!"* That is what we need to do in times of anxiety and depression. Gather with God's people and sing *"Spring up, O well!"*

Impacting The Environment

We must recognize that the problems within the ocean are the result of Man's actions. The sign of the rainbow which is being displayed worldwide for so many reasons, is in fact a universal covenant with God and Man that Jesus Christ is the only hope for change within the earth.

Now more than ever, we need to change our lifestyle. Each time we do the things that are wrong, it affects and impacts our environment. Each time a family is broken through divorce it impacts the environment, so we must restore the Family which is the First Line of Government. Ultimately, true change begins with salvation.

Climate Change is comprehensive, and it includes physical disasters, financial crises, curses, poverty – the environment is the key to addressing Climate Change! God wants us to be in a prosperous environment. He wants us to be in a peaceful environment. The climate that we need will only be achieved through the power of the Holy Spirit. Regardless of what we are going through, whether it be marital problems, business/economic problems, dry seasons, etc., once God intervenes, and there is a climate change; you will begin to walk in prosperity.

PRAYERS, DECREES AND DECLARATIONS

LET US PRAY

THE "NOW" PRAYER
(Inspired by Hebrews 11: 1)

Hebrews 11: 1 says, "Now faith is the substance of things hoped for, the evidence of things not seen."

By faith we believe we can get NOW miracles; not tomorrow, but NOW!

Father in the name of Jesus, I thank you for a NOW miracle in my body according to Isaiah 53. Let my Blood Pressure be 120 over 80, let my eyes have 20/20 vision, cause my immune, endocrine, respiratory, nervous systems, my thyroids and bones be in perfect working order. Remove every excess weight in my body in Jesus' name.

Let there be a NOW miracle in my finances according to Matthew 21: 22. I believe I receive uncommon financial miracles and provision from unknown sources. Let money find us each day.

Let there be NOW miracles in the signing of documents in my favor from governments, businesses, banks, grants, loans, contracts, transfer of assets to me.

Let there be NOW miracles in Real Estate Transactions – purchases and sales.

Let there be NOW miracles in our Consultation Services to business officials, governments, churches, media and entertainment.

Let there be NOW miracles for God's Grace, Favor, Gifts and Anointing.

Let there be a NOW miracle for our ministry and its members for increase.

Let there be NOW miracles for daily debt cancellation.

NOW, I command that all strongmen be removed, overthrown and evicted from our Sphere of Influence, whether demonic spirits or human beings.

I command that every door that has been closed by the enemy be opened NOW in the name of Jesus.

Let there be a NOW miracle according to Isaiah 58: 6, for yokes, bondage and oppression and all the impossible situations we are going through be broken NOW, and let the manifestation take place NOW! (Matthew 10: 27; Luke 18: 27)

Let there be a NOW miracle for all mountains and obstacles to be removed according to Jeremiah 32: 27 and Matthew 21: 27.

You are the God of the impossible and we command that each day the following words manifest on our behalf and in our favor:

Affirm, Acknowledge, Admit, Certify, Validate, Verify, Agree, Consent, Empathize, Approve, Authorize, Authenticate, Confirm, Accept, Contract, Permit, Adopt, Release, Favor, Sanction, Arbitration, Approbation, Insight, Wisdom, Substance, Knowledge, Impartation, Illumination, Transformation, Future, Prosperity, Grace, Anointing, Blessing, Fish, the Holy Spirit, Breakthrough, Understanding, Spiritual Gifts, Mercy and Compassion, New Wine, New Oil, New Grain, New Corn, Love, Souls, Joy, Healing, Deliverance, Discernment, Power, Rich, Peace, Pray, Worship, Forgiveness, Happiness, Solutions, Light, Hope, Increase, Stature.

Lord let those words NOW begin to manifest in our lives on a daily basis, and we thank you for a NOW answer, in Jesus' Name. AMEN!

DECREES AND DECLARATIONS

A Decree is a written announcement, declaration, command and word made in faith. Every royal decree is always followed by a proclamation. There is power in a decree. Righteous decrees bring victories, resources, change the atmosphere, reverse wicked decrees, shift into alignment, defeat the enemy, destroy opposition and bring revival.

PRAYER OF DECREES AND DECLARATIONS

"Yet Michael the archangel, in contending with the devil, when he disputed about the body of Moses, dared not bring against him a reviling accusation, but said, "The Lord rebuke you!" (Jude 1:9)

"And the Lord said to Satan, "The Lord rebuke you, Satan! The Lord who has chosen Jerusalem rebuke you! Is this not a brand plucked from the fire?" (Zechariah 3: 2)

In the name of Jesus Christ of Nazareth, the Lord rebuke you Satan! The Lord Who has chosen Jerusalem rebuke you from our lives, our assets, our household and from our breakthrough! We decree and declare that every unrighteous and un-Godly decree that has been decreed against (_____ Your Name____) is reversed, cancelled and been made null and void in Jesus' name.

We now make a new decree. According to Genesis 12 and Numbers 23: 23 which says <u>"For there is no sorcery against Jacob, nor any divination against Israel. It now must be said of Jacob and of Israel, 'Oh, what God has done!'"</u> no lying prophetic utterances against my family, our health, my ministry, my finance, my purpose, my victories, my breakthroughs and our support and inner circle.

In the name of Jesus, we make a new decree to recover from the enemy, everything that was stolen from us from false decrees and unrighteous declarations.

We decree that billions will come to us to establish Kingdom rule and Kingdom dominion in Real Estate, Finance, Politics, Business, Security, Education, Media, Entertainment, Medicine/Health/Pharmaceutical industries and even the wealth of the wicked will be transferred to us.

We make a new decree against the decrees made against the prosperity and success of our children and declare that our children shall be prosperous, successful and serve the Lord all the days of their lives and will grow in the Spirit of the Lord daily.

We decree that each day we will increase in wisdom, stature and favor with God and men according to Luke 2: 52.

We make a new decree against untimely death in our family and lineage, against infirmities and affliction, against the spirit of suicide, against the spirit of abortion, against the spirit of sabotage, against false accusations.

We decree that these new decrees will be executed by the angels of the Lord and there will be immediate consequences against anyone coming against this decree we now make today (___today's date___).

DECREE AGAINST ENEMY PLOTS

We declare that every wicked decree of the enemy, that has been decreed against us, shall not prosper. We make a new decree against that decree, that their decree against us shall be visited upon them. Every hole they have dug for us and every noose they have constructed to hang us shall be for them instead.

We decree that every lie, conspiracy and plot against our promotion shall come to naught and they shall be exposed instead. May the lies they have told about us be a quick exposure of them; and may their wealth be transferred to us from the four corners of the earth.

We decree that every decree against your marriage, health, finance, ministry, business and against every good thing the Lord has for us is null and void and we shall increase 1000-fold.

May the Esthers and Mordecais rise.

May there be new doors and greater access be ours.

May evil advisors begin to be shifted out of position and make way for those who are walking in truth and in God's will.

May the Vashtis be removed and the Esthers begin to rise.

May the poor and those who remain humble begin to rise.

May we be vindicated and promoted.

May every betrayer, every double agent, every person who undermines and every fifth column be exposed. Those who smile with us but stab us in the back, may they be exposed.

May favor and grace fill us so that we may walk in victory.

We decree all these decrees shall manifest now in Jesus' name!

PRAYER TO BREAK YOKES

Father in the name of Jesus, we ask Lord that You will break every past agreement and contract from ten generations. Break the Bastard Curse now in the name of Jesus, break witchcraft and immorality, break any agreement with spirit wives and sprit husbands, oppression, sickness and infirmities - break it! Break poverty and lack. Cut through and penetrate all evil forces, every cycle, stubborn problem, legal binding, failure at the edge of miracles, every spiritual padlock, cut it right now and release us. Intercept all satanic communication and bring confusion on all his agents transmitting on his behalf.

We break all the chains that the enemy used to keep us in bondage, we remove all demonic guards, we declare that angels will remove them, break the back of the enemy, destroy their devices and combination system, we break the cycle and every code that they may use against us. We bring an end to all satanic bondage on our life, city, and community, we break all satanic human network that is formed to stop my progress; let there be sudden destruction on all those who refuse to halt their attack against me, my family, my church. Those who rise up against me, let them cease to function. We command that they decompose and be separated into small components. Let any device that keeps us in yoke and bondage, break down and shut down. Destroy every oppressive agency that keep the people in bondage - agencies like political organizations, businesses, religious cult/occult, media, games, software and hardware, break them in Jesus' name. We command a revolt and a break away in the camp of the enemy and let there be breakthrough for our people in Jesus' name. Amen

PRAYER FOR HEALTH, HEALING, PROMOTION, PROTECTION, FINANCE AND GOD'S PRESENCE

There is no other God or any other realm Higher than GOD Who is the Most High God!

In the name of Jesus Christ of Nazareth, I declare Psalm 91 which says,

He who dwells in the secret place of the Most High shall abide under the shadow of the Almighty. I will say of the Lord, "He is my refuge and my fortress; my God, in Him I will trust." Surely He shall deliver you from the snare of the fowler and from the perilous pestilence. He shall cover you with His feathers, and under His wings you shall take refuge; His truth shall be your shield and buckler. You shall not be afraid of the terror by night, Nor of the arrow that flies by day, Nor of the pestilence that walks in darkness, Nor of the destruction that lays waste at noonday. A thousand may fall at your side, and ten thousand at your right hand; but it shall not come near you. Only with your eyes shall you look, and see the reward of the wicked. Because you have made the Lord, who is my refuge,

Even the Most High, your dwelling place, no evil shall befall you, nor shall any plague come near your dwelling; for He shall give His angels charge over you, to keep you in all your ways. In their hands they shall bear you up, lest you dash your foot against a stone. You shall tread upon the lion and the cobra, the young lion and the serpent you shall trample underfoot.

"Because he has set his love upon Me, therefore I will deliver him; I will set him on high, because he has known My name. He shall call upon Me, and I will answer him; I will be with him in trouble; I will deliver him and honor him. With long life I will satisfy him, And show him My salvation."

PRAYER FOR JAMAICA

Eternal Father, bless our land. Guide Jamaica with Your mighty right hand. Let our nation unite and be one. Break the Curse of Division that has been declared on the land by past generations. Let there be fair distribution of the nation's wealth and resources.

We pray that there shall be justice not only for the rich, but also for the poor, the fatherless and the widow. Break the cycle of poverty, manipulation, logic, pride, spiritual blindness, new age philosophies and the spirit of Leviathan from the land. Raise up leaders who will have a heart after God's own heart. Raise up those who will establish and build Your house

Almighty Father, begin to grant dreams and visions to the young and the old according to Joel 2, so that true prosperity will return to the Land. Break the spirits of abortion, sexual perversion, prostitution, crime, violence and other corruptions and release the spirits of Grace and Supplication over the nation. Begin to raise up new civil servants, politicians, business people, church leaders who have ~~the~~ mercy and compassion. Help the homeless and provide for them and grant them creative miracles.

Lord we ask You to break the bondage and stronghold of having only two political parties and raise up other parties. Break the spirit of oppression that exists over the nation and that the only spirit in control will be the Holy Spirit of God. Break the Bastard Curse from the people of the nation and let Family begin to be first priority again and the First Line of Government.

Lord, we thank You that those who diverted from the Cross will begin to return. We declare Jesus as Lord over our nation Jamaica and we reject any other religion or god presented to our nation. Lord, in the name, of Jesus Christ of Nazareth, overthrow every unjust law within the nation.

We decree Your peace and Your grace upon our island nation, so that Jamaica may, under God, increase in beauty, fellowship and prosperity, and play her part in the advancement of the welfare of the whole human race. Amen.

PRAYER FOR THE KEYS TO THE GATES

"And I will give you the keys of the kingdom of heaven, and whatever you bind on earth will be bound in heaven, and whatever you loose on earth will be loosed in heaven." (Matthew 16: 19)

You also said in Psalm 115: 15 – 16

"May you be blessed by the Lord, Who made heaven and earth. The heaven, even the heavens, are the Lord's; but the earth He has given to the children of men."

Father in the name of Jesus, we ask Lord for the Keys for the Gate of Real Estate, the keys for the Gate of the Supernatural, the keys to the Gate of the Kingdom of Heaven, the key to the Gate of Government, Private Sector and the different cities of the nation, the keys to the Gates to Governors in every city, every state, every parish and every province to which You have granted us access. We ask You Lord for the keys to the Gates of Sports – the NBA, the NFL, the NHL, Athletics Associations, Baseball Leagues, Golf Associations, and Soccer. We ask you for the Keys to the gates of Tourism, as well as the Keys for the Justice

System. We ask You also for the keys to the various levels of the Prophetic, which include insights, mysteries, doctrines and illumination. Lord we ask You for grace and favor.

We ask You for the keys to the Gates of (name every community, city, state, parish, country and region for You); as well as the keys of immigration, media, the United Nations, Israel, Jerusalem, the White House, Jamaica House, Buckingham Palace, Jerusalem, and current monarchies worldwide in addition to the World Bank and the IMF.

Lord please grant us the Keys to the Gates of healing, witty inventions, true wealth, ambassadorial keys as well as the Keys to the Gate of the Diplomatic circle.

Grant us the Keys to the Gate of Languages, Keys to the Gate of Finance, Wall Street, the Political Sector, the Economic Sector. Lord please grant us the keys even for areas we did not ask for but would help us fulfill our purpose for Your glory. Grant us keys to unlock dreams and visions; keys for signs, miracles and wonder and keys to the doors that will help us build Your church. In Jesus' name we pray, Amen.

PRAYER FOR THE BLOOD OF JESUS OVER YOUR FINANCES

Revelation 12: 11 says: "And they overcame him by the blood of the Lamb and by the word of their testimony, and they did not love their lives to the death."

Ephesians 1: 7 – 9 says: "In Him we have redemption through His blood, the forgiveness of sins, according to the riches of His grace which He made to abound toward us in all wisdom and prudence, having made known to us the mystery of His will, according to His good pleasure which He purposed in Himself"

(Hebrews 10: 19 - 22, Hebrews 12: 24, Ephesians 2: 13, 1 John 5: 6, 1 Peter 5: 7)

Instructions:

1. Declare this prayer each day over your money card or check book.

2. Ensure you spend wisely and know the balance and status of your account.

3. Pray over every money you receive.

4. Ask the Lord to direct you to be debt free

5. Follow instructions when the Holy Spirit speaks to you.

6. Write down all you owe on a sheet of paper and on the other side of that paper write these words, PAID IN FULL BY JESUS' BLOOD. He is our wealthy Benefactor. He has redeemed us and has taken our debts.

PRAY:

Father in the name of Jesus Christ of Nazareth, let Your Blood resurrect my finances! Destroy every debt that I owe. Destroy every legal right and curse from my finances. Stop every leak. Let the Blood of Jesus cause increase in my bank account – pouring money on money daily. Let the Blood of Jesus touch the hearts of people that they will give to me daily. Let it bring increase and business, sales and uncommon favor. Let the Blood of Jesus bring us into billionaire status, supernatural increase and deliverance. Cover my assets, increase my assets and open doors. Bring me in high places. Bring grace, favor and creative miracles. Let the blood of Jesus load us with benefits daily according to Psalm 68: 19.   Let the Blood of Jesus reveal Kingdom Principles and Economic strategies to me daily. Let the Blood of Jesus wipe out any and every late fee and high interest rate. Let the Blood of Jesus bring signs and wonders in my bank account.   Cover our information from attackers, hackers, witches and warlocks, in the name of Jesus Christ of Nazareth.   Let the Blood of Jesus cause bankers, politicians and millionaires to give into us. Let the Blood of Jesus cause companies to give into us. In Jesus' name we pray, Amen.

PRAYER FOR DIPLOMATIC IMMUNITY

The Diplomatic Immunity Prayer is for those on whom the enemy would want to use past issues to bring shame and reproach. This prayer will also destroy the Bastard Curse. Even if you are guilty in the past or present of any sin, God will forgive us and deliver us if we ask. We are diplomats, and we have the right and benefits of diplomatic immunity.

PRAY:

Father, in the name of Jesus, we thank You for covering, protection, favor and grace in all areas of our life daily with both Man and God. I thank You Lord for Diplomatic immunity and all the benefits of Diplomatic Immunity including Diplomatic Passport, Exemption from taxes and exemption from all court matters including Civil Law Suits. Thank You for Diplomatic Immunity from things from my past, even from past sins that I have committed.

As a Diplomat, according to Romans 10: 11, "You said whosoever believes in the Lord will never be ashamed.

According to Psalm 25: 1 – 7 "To You, O Lord, I lift up my soul. O my God, I trust in You; let me not be ashamed; let not my enemies triumph over me. Indeed, let no one who waits on You be ashamed; let those be ashamed who deal treacherously without cause. Show me Your ways, O Lord; Teach me Your paths. Lead me in Your truth and teach me, for You are the God of my salvation; on You I wait all the day. Remember, O Lord, Your tender mercies and Your loving-kindnesses, for they are from of old. Do not remember the sins of my youth, nor my transgressions; according to Your mercy remember me, for Your goodness' sake, O Lord."

According to Psalm 91: 1 – 6, "He who dwells in the secret place of the Most High Shall abide under the shadow of the Almighty. I will say of the Lord, "He is my refuge and my fortress; my God, in Him I will trust." Surely He shall deliver you from the snare of the fowler and from the perilous pestilence. He shall cover you with His feathers, and under His wings you shall take refuge; His truth shall be your shield and buckler. You shall not be afraid of the terror by night, nor of the arrow that flies by day, nor of the pestilence that walks in darkness, nor of the destruction that lays waste at noonday."

Lord, help us to carry out our Diplomatic assignments effectively and efficiently and we will only speak what our Divine Head of State instructs us to utter. Protect me and my family from every witchcraft, untimely death, curses, poverty, plagues, sins, sicknesses and diseases. Continue to grant us Kingdom asylum daily from the tongues and plots of men! Let Your Blood continue to wash and cleanse us daily; and cause us to see Diplomatic Immunity manifest upon and for us on a daily basis.

I thank You even now Lord, in Jesus' Name. AMEN.

PRAYER TO WIN THE WARS

Always sow a seed of $1000 as you pray this prayer

Father, in the name of Jesus, we ask Lord that according to Hebrews 1: 14, that my ministering angels be released and will go forth, so that Salvation will come to my household, my community and my family.

Psalm 68: 17 – 19 declares, "The chariots of God are twenty thousand, Even thousands of thousands; the Lord is among them as in Sinai, in the Holy Place. You have ascended on high, You have led captivity captive; You have received gifts among men, even from the rebellious, that the Lord God might dwell there. Blessed be the Lord, Who daily loads us with benefits, the God of our salvation!" We command the hosts of angels to carry out the functions of this Word.

Lord, let every contrary wind, storm, volcano, man, woman, animal, that comes against Your purpose, our lives or the vision be totally demolished. Release angelic hosts to demolish Sanballat, Tobiah, Geshem, Ahab, Jezebel, Absalom and every other demonic spirit including the four (4) hierarchies of the demonic realm.

Give us Spiritual insight to be ahead of our enemies. Bring confusion and madness in their midst. Destroy every device they are using against us and destroy their communication system and network! Give us victory as you have given to Barak, Debra and Joshua!

According to Psalm 103: 2, Let the angels that are assigned to me bring forth money, open doors of access, remove the head of every Goliath that stands before me, demolish every opposition, plot, trap or conspiracy, recover all stolen blessings and bring in the spoils to me. Lord, cause these angels to remove every guard standing at the high places and places of influence in order to keep God's people out, including media, financial sector, education, security, politics and real estate.

Bring down every empire that opposes us and let angels fight for the vision You have given us. Destroy all ancestral and familiar spirits. Let Your angels help us with the vision. Let Your power be demonstrated in our midst always. Let Your angels guide us into the Promised Land. As You have done for Daniel, give us 10 times more than the power the enemy. Anywhere there are blessings for us or documents to be signed and approved for us, cause Your angels to have it executed and bring the blessings to us.

We pray in Jesus' name. Amen.

PRAYER FOR QUICK TURNAROUND OF TRAVEL DOCUMENTS

Father, in the name of Jesus, I come to You right now for quick approval! You said in Your word the earth is the Lord's and the fullness thereof. Everything belongs to You! I decree and declare that You will release Your mightiest angels that specialize in travel documents for Your people.

We command those angels right now, to go forth for quick release of my travel documents! Passports – be signed now! Citizenships – be approved now! Residencies – be signed now! Birth Certificates – be signed and released now! Let every Satanic network conspiring to stop or delay us, or to bring us to shame, scatter and disintegrate now in the name of Jesus!

Lord, cause a shift and a shake that will cause us to get quick approval! Blind the open eyes that would want to come against my breakthrough; and open every blind eye that would bring favor to me.

Let your Spiritual bulldozer remove every blockage coming against my travel documents.

Remove plots, traps, stones, debris from my path that I will get quick access and approval. Overturn every delay right now.

Cover every travel document with the Blood of Jesus! Let goodness mercy, grace and favor manifest on my behalf.

I command every immigration officer, every inspector, counselor to release my documents now in the name of Jesus.

I bind the following spirits that would want to work against my cause: The Bastard Curse, Leviathan, Jezebel, Delay, Frustration, Mistake, Bad Luck, Logical and Analytical Mindsets, Strongholds, Lack and Fear. We bind them up with chains and shackles and we command victories! Promote those who would advance our cause; and transfer those in High Places that would want to frustrate the causes of God's people!

In Jesus' name I pray, Amen.

PRAYER FOR INCREASE AND AGAINST BACKLASH

From Psalm 50 & Psalm 24

Father, in the name of Jesus, we thank You for increase in all areas this week! Increase in Sales, Profit Margin, Favor, Joy, Peace, Health, Customers and Clients, Goodness and Mercy! Let Your Favor-Shield surround me daily; let it go before me daily.

I decree and declare Checks in the Mail, Debt Cancellation, Rebates, Reduction in Utility Bills, Reduction in Bank Charges, Favor with Bank Managers, Favor with City Officials, Favor with Security Personnel.

I decree and declare that my customers will be satisfied and they will be advertising my business wherever they go! God will supply all my needs according to His riches in glory by Christ Jesus.

I decree and declare that angels will go before us and bid on our behalf daily. I loose new establishments. I loose and command to be brought to me, property, assets, cars, houses, money, planes, jewelry, support personnel, Financial Resources and all other resources – spiritual and natural - that I require to accomplish God's will and purpose for the building of the His Kingdom and for our good. Show me Your way and teach me your paths daily. (Psalm 25: 5) Reveal Your secrets to me Lord and show me your covenant. (Psalm 25; 14)

Psalm 24:1 declares the earth is the Lord's and the fullness thereof and they that dwell therein. Everything on and in the earth belongs to you; and nothing is impossible. Let the impossible happen today on my behalf. Some trust in chariots and horses, but we will remember the name of the Lord our God! Let Your glory fall on me and my business.

Let Your Glory fill me, my household, my business and my life! We bind all territorial spirits! O Lord! How excellent is Your name in all the earth! Who has set Your glory above the heavens! Let your glory bring transformation daily.

I decree that we are blessed in the city, blessed in the country, blessed in our going out and our coming in! Whatever we touch is blessed – and because we are blessed, those who bless us will be blessed; those who curse us will be cursed.

Let every backlash against our success be a backlash upon the enemy instead! In Jesus' name we pray! AMEN.

THE BLOOD OF JESUS PRAYER

Father, in the name of Jesus. We have the Blood of Jesus right to come before the throne of Grace for blessing and protection.

Satan, you have no legal right to my Body, Soul or Spirit because Jesus already paid in full to set me free from Satanic bondage – Romans 3: 25 "Because of the Blood of Jesus, no curse can come to my finances and household. Right now, I plead the Blood of Jesus upon my household, Bank account and the perimeter of my home.

We plead the Blood of Jesus against any affliction by demonic or unclean spirits against my body, children, friends and family.

We plead the Blood of Jesus against death, hell and Hades.

We plead the Blood of Jesus upon all un-Godly past relationships, un-Godly past covenants and contracts; upon all past Common-Law relationships, fornications and adulteries and against any involvement in witchcraft by me or anyone using it against me.

I plead the Blood of Jesus against any abortion that we have committed spiritually or naturally in the past in Jesus' name.

Because of the power of the Blood of Jesus, I plead it against any diseases, plagues and viruses that would come against me, my household, my community, my school, my church and my country. (Exodus 12: 7, 13, 29 – 30)

I use the Blood of Jesus as a hedge around me, my household, my family and friends 24 hours per day, 7 days per week!

I use the blood also to purify me, that I may live holy and in righteousness.

I use the Blood of Jesus against all the ranks within the Satanic including witches, warlocks, Santeria, principalities and powers, rulers of darkness, wickedness in high places, the anti-Christ spirit, black magic and voodoo.

Let the Blood flush out of me any implantation within my body, any familiar or ancestral spirits coming against me and any bad dreams. I use the Blood of Jesus to dry up Leviathan's serpents and scorpions, as well as lies and accusations coming against me.

Cover me daily with your Blood Lord Jesus, let it bring deliverance in all areas of my life including areas where there is the spirit of bondage. Let it bring favor daily and let it cancel every debt, destruction, bad intention, deception and impure motives against our lives. Let the Blood of Jesus remove obstacles, hindrances and iron-like curses that come about through human or demonic influences and activities.

Let the Blood of Jesus wash away sins, curses, poisons, lying words against us;

Let the Blood of Jesus wash away plots, traps, viruses, germs;

Let the Blood of Jesus cancel all of Satan's plans concerning me.

Let the Blood of Jesus bring revival, refreshing, restoration, resurrection, success and prosperity, grace and favor in Jesus' name. AMEN!

PRAYER FOR COMPREHENSIVE PROSPERITY

Father, in the name of Jesus we come to You right now. Yahweh Rapha, the Most High Almighty El Elyon, El Shaddai, we come before You for the sake of prosperity and for the benefits You have promised us within Your Word regarding prosperity, and we are receiving it today, as Your Kingdom children, in 3 areas of our lives – financial, spiritual and health.

We thank You Lord, for riches, wealth, spiritual growth, restoration, and we further declare, according to Psalm 144: 12 – 15, "That our sons may be as plants grown up in their youth; that our daughters may be as pillars, sculptured in palace style; that our barns may be full, supplying all kinds of produce; that our sheep may bring forth thousands and ten thousands in our fields; that our oxen may be well laden; that there be no breaking in or going out; that there be no outcry in our streets. Happy are the people who are in such a state; happy are the people whose God is the Lord!"

Let everything be balanced in our lives that we will fulfill our purpose. All the organs in our bodies will function the way they were created to function. No organ will try to undermine any other organ. So we command order in our body, soul and spirit, heart, lungs, liver and kidneys, as well as our brains, immune system, blood, endocrine system, digestive system, thyroids and function according to God's original plan. I call all organs into accountability and command them to work in unity with each other. I call our eyes to be consecrated and we will look only on the clean things not the unclean things. Our ears will only hear the positive things. I call prosperity, protection and a balanced and fruitful life as you shower us with prosperity daily.

Grant us our daily quota that is allocated to us and let there be daily impartation of Your Presence, Your goodness, mercy and compassion. (Psalm 68: 9 & 18)

Bless all the works of my hands and cause me to prosper in all things. Bless my bread and my water, my seed and the fruit of my labor. Bless my storehouses and my bank accounts. Bless the city/town in which I live.

Bless me with miracle money so that I will be a blessing to others. Grace, favor and increase shall be my portion daily. Even my enemies will bless me, when they see the goodness of God upon me

El Shaddai, let multiplication – increase take place daily in my life. Expand our access and influence daily. Give us staff that will enhance us. According to Genesis 39: 2 – 3, be with us and prosper us and help us to have success in all things daily.

We claim Psalm 72: 16 upon our lives, and we stand on and claim the blessings of Psalm 34: 9 – 10 because we fear You and seek You – so we command and receive the best things from you today that we have all good things in our lives.

According to Proverbs 13: 22, we thank You for wealth transfer, ideas, wisdom, knowledge, favor and grace daily.

PRAYER TO CANCEL NEGATIVE Ds

Father, in the name of Jesus, we come to You right now, by Your Holy Spirit. We cancel all negative words that come against us that begin with the letter 'D'.

Cause us to have DOMINION daily over every earthly thing and situation. DELIVER us daily from every earthly and demonic force coming against us.

Help us to be DECISIVE and give us the DESIRE of our hearts. Help us Lord to receive the DEEP things of You.

Let Your DIVINITY take precedence over divination, lack, sickness and diseases! Let DOUBLE DOORS open to us daily!

Let Your DUNAMIS power manifest in our lives and let DEVELOPMENT and high DISCERNMENT take place daily. Let us be DIFFERENT, DISCIPLINED and DELIVER us from DANGER. Let us DWELL in Your Presence and DRINK at Your fountain. Let DRASTIC change take place in our lives and let us experience DELIVERANCE and not denial!

Remove delay and let new DISCOVERIES take place every day! Give us DRIVE and zeal! Let You DOVE manifest in our lives and let no termination or decrease take place in our lives. Dig up everything in our lives that was not planted by you; and cause us to walk in absolute DOMINION!

In Jesus' name! Amen.

PRAYER TO CALL THINGS INTO BEING

(Scriptural References: Romans 4: 17, Proverbs 18: 21, Mark 11, Hebrews 11: 1)

We have the authority to call things into being as though they were. We can create change in our environment. So, Lord,

I decree and declare that God's presence, grace and favor will manifest in my life on a daily basis.

I decree that souls from the four corners of the earth with established, wise, pure and stirred up hearts will come now to help us build.

I decree debt write-offs and continual abundance of cash flow will locate me daily.

I decree healing to my body, soul and spirit and upon my family daily. I call forth Kingdom businesses and Kingdom banks that I shall own in the name of Jesus and the wealth of the wicked shall be transferred to me in Jesus' name.

I decree the manifestation of the nine gifts of the Holy Spirit as well as accuracy, precision and clarity.

I call forth cash, assets and checks to me in abundance, as well as gold, silver, diamonds, rare gems, as well as unusual furniture and designer clothes and shoes.

I call forth luxury vehicles, lands and other properties for investment purpose. I call forth buildings for schools, church, humanitarian outreach, farming, television studios, and recording studios and declare that people shall show us grace and favor and bless us.

I decree that every mountain standing in our way shall become plains as I speak grace to them.

I decree that Your Kingdom people shall have a seat at the table of influence in Real Estate, Politics, Business, Government, Education, Security, Medicine, Agriculture, Immigration and Law/Justice.

I also call forth influence and power upon me over the fowls of the air, the fish of the sea and over every living thing that moves upon the earth. All the resources from the marine kingdom – according to Psalm 74 – is transferred to me now in Jesus' name and we call forth the resources according to Isaiah 60 shall be transferred to me and my family, because we have the legal right. Isaiah 2: 4 shall be our portion.

I declare it is so in Jesus' name. Amen.

PRAYER FOR THE POOR AND RIGHTEOUS

Jesus, Son of David, Have mercy! Remember the poor, the fatherless and the widow, the homeless, those without food, children who do not have any clean drinking water and those who have been raped and are being abused.

Cause a shift globally so that there will be equality in distribution. Provide the resources for Pastors and God-fearing people who have a heart or the poor that their vision will manifest.

Bring conviction to those who are wasting billions while there are many sleeping in their cars without a roof. You have seen the banks and those who are heartless - begin to raise up those entrepreneurs with a heart of flesh who have mercy and compassion so that they can revive the market.

Bring conviction to churches and pastors who are wasting billions on buildings and other things while people are dying of hunger within their gates.

Raise up those with wealth that would provide job and raise up politicians who will lead with grace, mercy and compassion.

Finally, Lord we pray for shifting and shaking within the globe that will benefit your people, in Jesus' name. Amen.

PRAYER FOR FAVOR AND GRACE

Father in the name of Jesus, I come to you right now asking You to let the Favor of God locate us today! Let it speak to us in all areas of our lives, and also in our physical body, our Church, our business, bank account. Let the favor of God speak on our behalf and cause the enemy to be silent concerning us.

Let the favor of God bring increase to us from both Man and God.

Let the Favor of God open doors for us in government, entertainment, media, security, financial institutions, sports and justice. In Jesus' name.

Let the Favor of God locate my address today and bring blessings, healing and deliverance and other resources.

Let the favor of God bring miracles, signs and wonders, contracts in sales, real estate, listings and all other kinds of contracts in Jesus' name.

Let the Favor of God break every generational curse and bring restoration in Jesus' name.

Everything that was stolen, restore now in Jesus' name.

Amen.

PRAYER TO BREAK YOKES OF BONDAGE AND OPPRESSION

(This Prayer is to undo, cut, loose, free, deliver, and break from bonds/bondage. Say it aggressively each day!)

Father in the name of Jesus, we ask You to break separate and damage any agreements and past covenants with any evil or evil organization. I refuse to observe any agreement from any covenant that I have ever made with Satan in the past. I break it in Jesus' name. Satan has no legal right to impose any past agreement and contract because of the shed blood of Jesus. The contract I have with Jesus makes all contracts I have with Satan null and void!

I cancel any contract that I have through any association or that anyone of my maternal or paternal ancestors have made that would invoke any curses – generational, ancestral or bastard curses! Break any curses that have come through sexual immorality, witchcraft, oppression, sickness, infirmities, poverty, cycle, stubborn problems or failure at the edge of a miracle. Cut through and penetrate all evil forces – spiritual or physical - whether they be principalities and powers, rulers of darkness, wickedness in high places, gates, chains or chords that are holding my blessings back.

I pray, Holy Spirit, which You will break and interrupt all satanic communications and bring confusion on all his agents. I break the back of the enemy that holds us in bondage. I break down all demonic guards! I break their ranks also, their codes, combinations and cycles that keep us in poverty and bondage. I bring to an end, all satanic yokes, and bondage on our lives, cities, communities and nation! I undo all oppressive systems of government and business, including satanic and human networks to stop our progress and the enhancement of God's Kingdom, our ministry and our household.

Let there be sudden destruction upon all who refuse to stop the attacks upon us. Let every system that rises up against me cease to function. Let any device that keep us in yokes and bondage decompose and separate into small components. Shut down and breakdown any oppressive agencies, secret memorandums or secret deals, whether it be political, economic religious, cultic/occult, movies, media, video games, technological.

Break all yokes of oppression that keep us in bondage; whether it be racism, classism or any other prejudices. Let there be a breakaway in the camp of the enemy!

LET THERE BE SUDDEN BREAKTHROUGH FOR ME RIGHT NOW!

Break all chains, bonds, chords or negative words concerning me - right now, in Jesus' name. AMEN!

PRAYER TO BREAK BASTARD CURSE

Father in the name of Jesus, I ask for forgiveness for my lineage from ten generations for myself and my family. We stand on Galatians 3: 13. We put all curses associated with the Bastard Curse that are coming against my purpose whether it be abortion – natural or spiritual; murder, death, incest, lust, rejection, failure at the edge of miracle, alcohol, hatred, bitterness, rejection. We ask You Jesus that You will wipe away all sins and curses, every red circle against my name, every opposition, we replace it with God's grace and we renounce the Bastard Curse, we take back all legal rights from the enemy.

Lord, in the name of Jesus Christ of Nazareth, we close all portals. Erase and delete all satanic records from the past regarding any affairs of my life and we speak new beginning in Jesus name. Remove any blockage known and unknown, any legal rights and I command that I will begin to advance. Lord we break the bastard curses now from my life. Begin to enlarge my territory like Jabez in Jesus name (2 Chronicles 4: 10). We remove all legal rights and covenants in Jesus name and we thank You Lord for victory as You cleanse my spiritual DNA with Your blood. I declare, no more blocking of my progress and advancement, no more delays, in Jesus' name. Amen.

PRAYER FOR 3 AREAS OF PROSPERITY

1.   Pray in tongues (your spiritual language) daily.
2.   Pray the Psalms daily.
3.   Say a Prayer of Thanksgiving daily.

Study these Scriptures as well.

Psalm 23, Psalm 72, Psalm 103, Psalm 112, Psalm 121, Psalm 144, Matthew 6: 9 – 13

God wants to bless us in three main (3) areas:

1.   Financially
2.   Health-wise
3.   Spiritually

We must be balanced. Many times, we prosper spiritually while we struggle health-wise and financially; or many millionaires may be prospering financially, but they are poor in spirit and in health. This prayer, as you pray it each day and walk in obedience to God's instructions. (Deuteronomy 28: 1 – 14). Read God's Word daily and honor Him with your finance (Malachi 3)

PRAY:

Father, in the name of Jesus, I come to You Lord to pray for financial breakthrough right now. We call forth money from the four corners of the earth. We call in all vows and money owed to us. We thank You for money-yielding ideas.

We ask Lord for wisdom and wealth. Give gold, silver and people who will help ups financially for the vision You have given us.

Lord we pray for perfect health daily.

Give us revelation with the right food to eat and provide the resources to purchase the right food.

Heal us Lord, spiritually, naturally and emotionally. We thank You for blessings in three (3) areas of our life.

Bless the work of our hands in Jesus' name. Amen.

Pray Without Ceasing!

BIBLIOGRAPHY

https://books.google.com/books?id=ACYzDwAAQBAJ&pg=RA1-PA302&lpg=RA1-PA302&dq=Swiss+and+German+Scientists+the+sun+is+brighter&source=bl&ots=gA8ullO8wz&sig=ACfU3U1V6yz6bWpMo7OTo0EFL9gB1BnxOQ&hl=en&sa=X&ved=2ahUKEwjWkMmap6vjAhXOZs0KHUYaBWIQ6AEwFHoECAkQAQ#v=onepage&q=Swiss%20and%20German%20Scientists%20the%20sun%20is%20brighter&f=false

http://fathers.com/statistics-and-research/the-consequences-of-fatherlessness/2/

https://www.government.nl/topics/embassies-consulates-and-other-representations/diplomatic-immunity

Made in the USA
Monee, IL
22 March 2021